LEARNING RESOURCES CTR/NEW ENGLAND TECH.
GEN   PN6147.S3
Schaeffer, N   The art of laughter /

3 0147 0000 7769 6

PN6147 .S

Schaeffer,

The Art of laughter

The Art of Laughter

The Art
of
Laughter

NEIL SCHAEFFER

COLUMBIA UNIVERSITY PRESS
New York

Chapter 4 of this book appeared in 1976 under the title "Lenny Bruce without Tears" in *College English* 37, no. 6. Thanks are due to the editors for permission to reprint.

Library of Congress Cataloging in Publication Data

Schaeffer, Neil, 1940–
The art of laughter.

Includes bibliographical references and index.
1. Wit and humor—History and criticism. 2. Wit
and humor—Philosophy. I. Title.
PN6147.S3 809.7'009 81-3807
ISBN 0-231-05224-3 AACR2

Columbia University Press
New York   Guildford, Surrey

Copyright © 1981 Columbia University Press
All rights reserved
Printed in the United States of America

10 9 8 7 6 5 4 3 2

*Clothbound editions of Columbia University Press books
are Smyth-sewn and printed on permanent and durable
acid-free paper.*

For
Sheldon Bach

Acknowledgments

I am grateful for the help of Wayne C. Booth and John Middendorf, and for the abiding influence of the memory of James L. Clifford.

Contents

The Art of Laughter

Introduction

THE TASK I have set for myself is to develop a general theory that accounts for laughter and for the less vocal pleasures that are associated with laughter. The field for this kind of pleasure is quite wide, including such specialized genres as the comic novel and dramatic comedy, as well as verbal and practical jokes, and the kind of adventitious or natural events which cause laughter seemingly without human intervention or design.

My aim will be to discover the definitive factors which are common to all of these related literary and natural events, and also to define the psychical mechanisms which permit these events to have their well-known effects, laughter or the pleasure associated with laughter. It will be seen that the defining feature both of the external stimulus and of the mental process that yields these pleasures is the force of context. What I come to term the "ludicrous context" is an aspect neither of the content nor of any particular style of an event that occasions laughter. Rather, it is a set of cues or instructions embedded in or imposed upon a particular event, whether literary or natural, that stimulates a parallel mental state of ludicrousness in the observer.

It will be seen that one of my presumptions in this kind of analysis is that any given event is subject to an infinite range of interpretation depending entirely upon the instructions presumed to be contained in or imposed upon that event. Such a range may be generated in each case by slightly changing or differently stressing the factors in the set of instructions, that is, by minutely changing the context in which the event is to be reinterpreted. While it may be reasonable to reject most of the meanings so generated as injudicious, implausible, anachronistic, irrational, etc., and indeed, such judgments usually deserve our concern, it is important that in doing so we are consciously aware that we are making biased decisions in rejecting most and approving only some of the infinite sets of possible reading instructions. For our particular interest in comedy, it pays to understand what minimal and definitive set of instructions must be present in an event or imposed upon it from the outside in order that we may respond to it with laughter or with the pleasure associated with laughter. It is from this perspective that I offer to define what invokes laughter and to examine individual works of comedy.

A particular value of the idea of context is that it refers not only to the set of instructions associated with the event, but also to the parallel mind-set or state of mind capable of carrying out those instructions and responding to that event. In presenting context as the definitive feature of laughter, I offer a bridge between the psychological and the rhetorical approach to the problem, and I also avoid the difficulties and illogicalities of the traditional rhetorical approach, which has unsuccessfully attempted to define comedic events in terms of a special ludicrous content or a special ludicrous style, or a combination of both. If I am successful in adducing to the idea of the ludicrous context only those few defining features which together account for laughter, then I will have created a theoretical method for unifying the genres and events which produce laughter and the pleasures associated with laughter. In addition to developing a field theory of laughter, I will also offer in the defining features of the ludicrous context a means of analyzing the nature of a particular ludicrous context, that is, the particular set of instructions with which individual works of the comic spirit achieve their own special quality of laughter. My aim, then, is two-fold: to establish the idea of the ludicrous context, and to show how that context is elaborated and itself becomes a fruitful subject for analysis in individual works of the comic spirit.

CHAPTER ONE

Matter and Manner:
Theories of Laughter

L AUGHTER IS, of all the expressions of mind and heart, the most
enigmatic. It poses a special problem for the critic of literature:
if it is not clear why or at what people laugh in nature, it is equally
unclear how or why certain artful productions effect the same response. The subject remains obscure, but not for want of clarifiers.

The theories of laughter fall into two mutually exclusive interpretations. According to one, there is in human nature an active capacity
for creating humor upon the world around it. In such a view, the
artist actively distorts reality in such a way as to evoke laughter. This
is the interpretation of all those who discover a dangerous or potentially dangerous tendency in the art of laughter.[1] Humor, in this view,
is a capacity that ought to be limited, just as the devoted are com-
manded against uttering the Lord's name in vain. The temptation to
play with names is real enough, as any child, whose main business
is to learn the names of things, knows. Is there any real significance
in the fact that in English God spelled backwards is dog? Or is there
any real meaning in the fact that the name of a child's enemy can be
changed by the transposition of a letter or two into the word for some
ignominious quality ("Stewart/stupid")? The comparisons so generated are utterly invidious. Yet they please; they can make us laugh
with pleasure. The apparent danger is that while the meaning is
spurious, it can survive, as in nicknames, with a tenacity stronger
than truth. So a suspicion arises against those who make reality laughable by the effort of their imaginations. Critics unsympathetic to
laughter tend to view the act of making something laughable as an
imposition of a ludicrous style upon the serious content of reality and

as an incitement to the potentially antisocial or even sinful emotions of pride, scorn, and anger.

On the other side, the defenders of laughter tend to rely upon the theory that sees laughter as an appropriate human response to whatever is inherently laughable in reality. In this view, the imagination is fairly passive, merely responding to events. Whenever the laughable presents itself in nature, a person *must* laugh, willy-nilly. Aristotle, for example, felt that we must laugh when we see painless deformity.[2] The point is that this theory of the laughable removes in large part the responsibility from the laugher and places it upon the laughable object itself. This would be a pretty good defense against the critics of laughter were it possible reliably to identify the laughable in nature with enough exclusivity to separate it from the serious in nature. But this defense fails if it turns out that laughter is a function of style rather than of a ludicrous content in nature.

If laughter is, in fact, a matter of style, anything could be made laughable. Indeed, what could a resolute jester *not* laugh at? As one critic put it, "A horse-laugh set up by a circle of fox-hunters, would overpower the best poet or philosopher whom the world ever admired."[3] If anything can be made laughable, then ludicrousness would appear to be rather a style than a thing, an application that can be imposed indiscriminately on any aspect of reality rather than something inherent in only certain parts of it. Aleksandr I. Solzhenitsyn records a particularly perverse example of paranoia over the secret meaning of laughter and its power to subvert truth. He tells about the imprisonment of a Russian citizen who, while reading *Pravda*, smiled:

> He had been imprisoned for a *facial crime* (really out of Orwell)—for a *smile!* He had been an instructor in a field engineers' school. While showing another teacher in the classroom something in *Pravda*, he had smiled! The other teacher was killed soon after, so no one ever found out *what* Orachevsky had been smiling at. But the smile *had been observed*, and the fact of smiling at the central organ of the Party was in itself scacrilege![4]

To repeat, critics of laughter tend to think of laughter as the effect of a ludicrous style which is capable of corroding even the most pure, true, and sacred object with derisive jesting; its defenders, on the other hand, portray laughter as a thoroughly appropriate reaction to ludicrous objects. Eighteenth-century English apologists of laughter, for example, liked to slightly misinterpret Lord Shaftesbury and claim that laughter was a test of truth: if you can laugh at something, then it was not quite pure in the first place.[5]

The question remains: is ludicrousness in nature or in the eye of the laugher? When critics and philosophers speak of the ludicrous in nature or reality, what we understand them to mean is that there is in reality some thing, or some relationship of things which makes people laugh (admitting that a particular individual may not laugh because he never laughs, or because, although he laughs at other things, he never does at that particular thing, or because, although he generally laughs at that thing, he just does not feel like laughing at it, or perhaps at anything, at that particular moment). We are talking then, about a ludicrous thing, or some relationship of ludi-crous things in reality, and the capacity of human nature to respond to it with laughter. There can be nothing in nature that can be termed purely ludicrous without reference to the human nature that so per-ceives and laughs at it—any more than there can be beauty or ugli-ness, order or chaos, without the same reference. For those are terms and ideas that reflect the human interest and perspective in reality, not the interest of reality itself. We are too self-possessed ever to be able to know what interest reality has in itself. We can not even agree on a universal view of our own interest. What is beautiful to the landscape painter may not be to the farmer. As attractive and as logical an alternative as it might seem for critics to conclude that there must be an object in nature termed the ludicrous, there remains the difficulty of reaching a definition that can successfully ignore human nature and that includes all objects in nature that can cause laughter and excludes all those that do not.

The debate may begin to be resolved by first agreeing that a single object in nature cannot be the sole cause of laughter. If it were true, comedians would not pay for jokes; they would merely provide them-selves with a platypus, or whatever object proved ludicrous, and silently display it before audiences for laughs. It would seem then that while no single object is laughable in itself, it may be made so by the manner in which it is presented to us. Once we admit the modification of a ludicrous manner, we are no longer speaking about a single ludicrous object in nature. It is in this somewhat more complicated light that Aristotle viewed the ludicrous as a "species of ugliness; it is a sort of flaw and ugliness which is not painful or injurious."[6] For Aristotle, the ludicrous object is clearly not a single object, but rather a kind of ugliness qualified by its characteristic effect—laughter rather than the expected pain. In looking for the source of ludicrousness in nature, Aristotle still had to fall back for the crucial element in his definition upon human nature and the definitive laughing response. While he did supply the interesting concept of ugliness, he still resorted to the circularity so common to thinking on this subject: the laughable is that which makes us laugh. And we are no wiser than before. Exact definition in this matter inevitably turns away from general nature to human nature, and critics who employ the term, "the ludicrous," really comment on the latter rather than the former.

Yet there are obviously ludicrous events that occur in the natural world—occur, that is, without human intervention. The term natural humor I apply to such events, objects, and contexts in the natural world that inspire us to laughter. They are in contrast to artful humor, all those events, objects, and contexts which we actively employ to cause laughter. One might have to wait a long time for this pleasure were he dependent solely upon the natural variety. After all, how many times each day do the materials of reality naturally arrange themselves in just the exact juxtaposition and with just the right timing or manner necessary to stimulate laughter? How often does a pail full of water perch, without human intervention, atop a door? We would be a pretty humorless tribe were we limited only to this adventitious or natural laughter. Artful humor is an imitation of and an improvement upon natural laughter, sophisticating and complicating the natural variety with all the skill of art and at the same time rendering it convenient and replicable.

Whether the laughter is raised naturally or artfully, the fact remains that there is in nature no single object that is of and by itself ludicrous. Virtually every definition of the ludicrous depends upon the concept of incongruity and juxtaposition. But nature consists of an infinitude of juxtapositions. Near the tree is a flower. Around the flower grass grows. We perceive these relationships as normal. If, for a moment, we were to consider nature as the author of all the things and their relationships in reality, how would we characterize her work? Let us say that reality, viewed as if it were a work of art, presents itself as being realistic in the sense that no one mode or genre predominates. At different times and places, and in its various appearances, real life may be reduced by human perception to seem tragic, or lyric, or comic, or pastoral, or ironic—whatever. But in its fullness, reality is a complexly mixed genre. The literary genres come into being as a means of separating, describing, and purifying our different responses to this complex blend of reality. So when the human artist copies nature, he must perforce copy only some limited aspect of her infinitely complex artistry: Nature as pastoral poet; Nature as tragic dramatist; Nature as comedian.

From the point of view of nature, there are no real incongruities. It is only from our human point of view that we imagine nature as comedian arranging incongruities for our pleasure. There is, for example, nothing incongruous about sea gulls and flying fish. They each pursue the interests of their separate natures within the context of general nature. Yet a photograph capturing a sea gull and a flying fish passing in flight would stand a chance of being considered a humorous incongruity—not, surely, by the creatures themselves, for their relatives had passed thus countless times for millenia. The event is of significance only to man, who extracts it from the flux of reality with his observation and who perhaps gives it even greater significance and permanence by photographing it or otherwise preserving it for his own and others' later pleasure. The event, the sudden juxtaposition of these two creatures, has given him pleasure, and not incidentally, perhaps even causally, it contains a significance, a meaning for him. Perhaps he sees in the bird's expression a theatrical double-take, or imagines the bird's surprise at seeing this strange creature, apparently neither fish nor fowl, flying by. Without exploring now the whole question of how far it is possible, or whether it is possible at all, to determine the intellectual content of a joke, it suffices to say that the juxtaposition of incongruous elements appears to contain a significance even if we are unable or unwilling to state precisely what it is.

Nothing could be more important in our appreciation of incongruity, and especially ludicrous incongruity, than the process of mental association. Every image, word, and thing excites in us a process of association which is conducted on many levels. This process is especially extensive as well as profound when the stimulus is significant, or when it is made so by incongruity or other intensifying features of its context. For example, when an image strikes our mind it is convenient to assume that one direction of the train of association will be a downward vertical, a symbol which represents a process of association away from the conscious stimulus towards more secret, elusive, and finally unconscious associations. It is also convenient to assume that another train of association will be horizontal, which may be pictured as irradiating from a center which is the original stimulus. These horizontal trains of association (one or many) make contact not with more secret images, but with images of about equal conscious value to the original stimulus. That is, the horizontal trains lead toward associations of equal categorical value to the original stimulus, while the vertical trains, whether springing from the original stimulus or developing out of the new categorical associations, lead toward deeper specificity and personal meaning. Our experience of each image is an extremely complex event, as wide-ranging and profound lines of thought and feeling are activated or at least sensitized. Each mental event, therefore, has a topographical extension along the horizontal plane and an archaeological extension down the verticals.

This model is useful for aesthetic, if not neurological, experience. When we say that a work of art is significant and may be read by many different kinds of people in different eras and on many different levels at once, we could use this model to help explain our common experience. A single image may, therefore, have a range of categorical associations and a range of potentially personal associations in depth. This is, then, a model that can be used for the mental process involved in aesthetic experience, both for incongruities in general, and for those special ludicrous incongruities that are the apparent cause of laughter.

While it must be true that the process of association occurs constantly in response to our experience, it would appear that this process is given an urgency by incongruity. An incongruity is a perceived juxtaposition of apparently unrelated ideas or things. We must presume that there is a degree of juxtaposition and a quantity of unrelatedness that we regularly treat as normal, so that a bowl containing different fruits appears to us as normal, while one containing, among the pears and bananas and apples, a sea urchin, strikes us as an example of incongruous juxtaposition, and intrudes upon our normal state of consciousness, demanding special attention and an unusual effort of understanding. With incongruity we see two things which do not belong together, yet which we accept at least in this case as going together in some way. That is, when we notice something as incongruous, we also simultaneously understand it to be in some minor way congruous.[7] Our mental task is to find this slender element of congruity amid the predominating elements of incongruity. When we do discover it, we feel satisfaction. I emphasize this point: we accept a minor principle of congruity at the precise moment that we recognize incongruity, for the latter would not have been characterized as incongruity in the first place without our immediate, simultaneous sense of a potential and hidden congruity. In other words, incongruities do have a kind of meaning, and this meaning is essential to our defining and noticing incongruity in the first place. For events, objects, and ideas which have absolutely no significant meaning whatsoever when juxtaposed we do not call incongruities. Rather, we treat them as irrelevancies. They do not command our attention, if we call them to our attention at all.

The kind of mental process we use to discover the meaning, significance, or congruity within incongruity may seem logical. We compare the two elements in the juxtaposition in order to determine what even slender thread binds such diversity together. To be sure, the logical capacity of our conscious mind plays its role here, but it is not our only resource, and it is probably not even our major resource for discovering the answer to the riddle. After all, it was not our logical consciousness that noticed the fact of incongruity in the first place. Rather, the incongruity broke into our thoughts. Suddenly we felt an incongruity (and the implicit secret congruity), and at that moment we knew no more than that. The fact of incongruity (and all that it means), is experienced instantaneously. Our noticing it is not a product of rational thought, nor can our experience of it be said to contain any significant process of discursive reasoning.

If the tie that associated the two incongruous objects is not the product of rational logic, the method that unravels the riddle is not a rational one either. It is not contrast alone that makes for incongruity. If that were the case, everything would appear incongruous, for no two things, even two of the "same" things, are really alike. Therefore, very similar things may become the poles of an incongruity, and quite dissimilar things may not be seen as incongruous. An incongruity is a contrast that triggers a significantly hidden meaning. If the act of generating or even apprehending the presence of an incongruity is not logical or necessarily conscious, the process of appreciating it need not be logical or conscious either. We discover the significance by the same method of association that generated it.

The point I want to make clear is that this deliberate process of analyzing an incongruity is much slower and more tentative than the process that generated it. There, the incongruity leapt into our consciousness, without necessarily requiring any preparation on our part to see or create it. In the after-experience of incongruity, we know and feel that something significant has occurred in our mind, but we do not know exactly what it is. We have a tense notion that we know more than we know, and we preserve this uncertain feeling as a means of arousing and sustaining our curiosity for the search. We could, of course, forget about the whole matter by saying that it is not important, or that it was only a feeling, or we may try to be satisfied with only the felt pleasure of the still unconscious significance of the event. But the brave and curious mind attempts to preserve the uncertain feeling as a stimulus for the work ahead. Keeping this feeling in the middle, the mind attempts to probe the trains of feeling and idea that emanate from the two poles of the incongruity in an effort to discover the significant tie that joins them. This is an attempt to call to consciousness a mental event which has already been completed and enjoyed, and whose energy has already been spent in the unconscious mind. To some, the search may appear as vain as looking for fire by raking last week's ashes. But means do exist for finding the significance of an incongruity, and they are as follows: the conventional meanings of the two poles of the incongruity; the meanings as modified by the context in which the incongruity appears; and our rational judgment, which correlates the imaginative evidence accumulating around both poles.

This work is an effort to recall to rational consciousness our original, almost entirely emotional, nonrational experience of the incongruity, for in our original experience we saw the polarity and also felt the disguised sameness or significance, because both factors had to be present for us to call the matter an incongruity in the first place. But, it may be asked, why torture the metaphor with intellectual tools when we felt it all the first time through? The effort of recall aims at purifying, expanding, categorizing, analyzing, personalizing the original experience. It begins with a conscious effort to recall by reactivating the train of associations that the incongruity originally inspired. This effort yields a great deal of psychological evidence which is always relevant to ourselves and may only in a very small way be relevant to the incongruity.

When a reader attempts to employ too much of this evidence prematurely, or to employ it indiscriminately in analyzing the incongruity, he is guilty of "reading into" the incongruity. Actually, reading into, as opposed to reading passively, is an essential, but must not be the final, act of criticism. Reading into obtrudes obviously private, necessarily idiosyncratic trains of association upon the original stimulus. The aim of the conscientious critic is to correlate these private evidences with the original stimulus in order to understand and explain not so much himself as it. It should be plain that metaphoric incongruity as it occurs in a poem, for example, limits the range of reading into, for any explanation of the mechanism of one poetic incongruity, one metaphor, must not only explain it, but also must be supported by the explanations of the other incongruities, the other metaphors, in the larger context of the poem. *A single incongruity is therefore more open to idiosyncratic interpretation than several incongruities that share a common context.*

I emphasize the above assertion because it will prove essential in answering the crucial question: what distinguishes ludicrous incongruity from other forms—poetic metaphors, for example—that do not produce laughter? Scholars of the laughable have observed that incongruity alone cannot be a complete definition of the ludicrous, for there are more incongruities that do not cause laughter than do. Those critics who observe this insufficiency of definition may add a discriminating stylistic modifier, generally "sudden"—sudden incongruity.[8] Laughter might seem to require a quickness of style, a turn that takes us by surprise and startles us into laughter. There is no doubt that the style of a joke is distinct from the style of a poem, yet it is difficult to calculate the degree of suddenness that distinguishes poetic from comic incongruity. Indeed, it is not a question of suddenness at all, because poetic incongruity may be just as sudden and surprising as ludicrous incongruity. Therefore, although suddenness may be a special feature of both kinds of incongruity, it is not a distinguishing feature of either.

An important clue that does distinguish ludicrous from poetic incongruities lies in the manner we read and read into them. There is no form of literature more unfriendly to rational analysis than the incongruity that causes laughter. Of course, laymen and beginning students are none too keen to apply rational analysis to any form of literature. They often feel that study will spoil the poem. Swift said, satirically, "Last Week I saw a Woman *flay'd*, and you will hardly believe, how much it altered her Person for the worse."[9] But if students are reluctant to analyze poetic incongruity, they tend absolutely to balk at analyzing the ludicrous variety. Whole classes will refuse even to begin analyzing a joke they all laughed at moments before. It is impossible to find out why they laughed, they claim. They stand upon Constitutionally sacred ground and defend their right to pursue happiness without the intervention of analysis.

Freud has contributed more than any other critic to our understanding of the psychological mechanism of our response to ludicrous events. His contribution here is an elaboration of his original discovery of the unconscious. According to Freud, a joke or witticism, that is, a ludicrous incongruity, begins to arouse ideas and pleasures that are normally repressed in the unconscious. However, the joking style of the presentation, the "joke-work," as he called it, indicates that the matter is not to be taken seriously so that the energy which would in a serious case have gone towards repression may now be spent in the pleasure of laughter. Laughter, then, in this view, is an aspect of the negative energy of repression.[10] This view of laughter as a saving in the economy of repression may be too negative. It is certainly a view that would not be acceptable to those who regard laughter as a positive response to the ludicrous in nature and in art. Moreover, the psychological mechanism that yields laughter remains in dispute. Why, for example, does a saving in repressive energy produce, of all possible human responses, laughter? What is not in dispute is that ludicrous incongruity has the capacity for initiating trains of association that proceed quickly into the unconscious mind. Our laughter may be a window, quickly opened and as quickly shut, into our unconscious mind. And it is this possibility in laughter for a profound and dangerous self-revelation that makes us defensive about probing into the event.

If a ludicrous incongruity has the capacity of exciting a train of ideas that proceeds through conscious into unconscious associations, why may not the same be said of serious or nonludicrous incongruities? Indeed, the same may be said of both. Our unconscious responses are not shut off when we read a serious poem. The mechanism of association is exactly the same whether we respond to an incongruity in a lyric poem or one in a joke. So it would appear that we have reached another dead end, except for the fact that I suggested earlier—namely, that while the range and depth of associations we might have to a particular incongruity or metaphor is potentially enormous, the range is in practice limited by the context in which that metaphor appears. Poetic metaphors adjust their potential meanings in a context of other ideas and other metaphors. This fact coincides with our common-sense experience that it is more likely for a class of students to arrive at a probable interpretation of a poem than of a joke. So the psychological processes of association initiated by both ludicrous and nonludicrous incongruity are exactly the same in kind. The difference between them, therefore, is not one of quality, but quantity. Ludicrous incongruities simply have the potential of inspiring a wider and deeper range of association.

It should be clear that the more associations that accrue around and down from each pole of the incongruity, the more possibilities exist for entirely personal, idiosyncratic significances or linkages between the two poles. And ludicrous incongruity initiates the widest possible range of idiosyncratic signification, whereas the number of linkages between the poles of a serious metaphor is limited by the presence of other metaphors. Of course, the layman may read into serious metaphors entirely idiosyncratic linkages and significances. This possibility exists, but it is not encouraged by the context. Ludicrous incongruities, on the contrary, tend positively to encourage the widest and deepest possible idiosyncractic interpretation. To put the issue bluntly, serious incongruities belong to a relatively closed system, while ludicrous incongruities belong to a relatively open system of signification. Hence, our common sense of the matter is again confirmed: it would indeed be impossible to interpret a joke with the same degree of certainty or probability that we expect and achieve in our interpretations of, for example, poetry.

We have been noticing an important difference in the effects of these two different kinds of incongruity: in ludicrous incongruity there is a wider range of association and a greater number of especially idiosyncratic linkages or significances. We are also nearer to finding the cause of this effect, but this is a very complex enterprise. Critics from Plato and Aristotle on have sought the genius of laughter in either an essentially ludicrous content or a ludicrous style, or sometimes, as with Freud, in a combination of both. If the genius or motive agency of the ludicrous is not to rest on some aspect of style, then we should be able to find it in the content of the incongruity. On the face of it, this may seem a likely possibility. We feel that there ought to be a functional aspect in the content; there ought to be some distinguishing characteristic in the contents of ludicrous incongruities. As much as we would like and as hard as critics have sought to discover a defining feature in the actual subject matter of ludicrous incongruities, none has been found that fully answers the exclusivity requirements of precise definition. That is, the problem is to find a kind of subject matter that is always present in ludicrous incongruity and is never present in nonludicrous incongruity.

Thomas Hobbes made an interesting attempt at defining the ludicrous content as pride, but he was careful also to attach a stylistic modifier, "sudden": "Sudden glory is the passion which makes those grimaces called laughter, and is caused by some sudden act of their own that pleases them or by the apprehension of some deformed thing in another, by comparison whereof they suddenly applaud themselves."[11] As provocative as Hobbes' contribution is, it was easily challenged, even ridiculed, as in this attack by James Beattie:

If Laughter arose from pride, and that pride from a sudden conception of some present eminency in ourselves, compared with others, or compared with ourselves as we were formerly; it would follow,—that the wise, the beautiful, the strong, the healthy, and the rich, must giggle away a great part of their lives, because they would every now and then become suddenly sensible of their superiority over the foolish, the homely, the feeble, the sickly, and the poor;—that one would never recollect the transactions of one's childhood, or the absurdity of one's dreams, without merriment;—that in the company of our equals we should always be grave;—and that Sir Isaac Newton must have been the greatest wag of his time.[12]

Despite the heat of the debate, we still feel that a good critic ought to be able to strike a balance between the topical and stylistic factors in ludicrousness.

Freud tried to pursue both approaches, but he also noted "the fact that we receive from joking remarks a total impression in which we are unable to separate the share taken by the thought content from the share taken by the joke-work."[13] "Strictly speaking," he added, "we do not know what we are laughing at."[14] In practice, even if it is difficult, perhaps impossible to divide accurately the factors of thought and style in a particular joke, Freud, more than any other critic, made the best attempt theoretically to distinguish the subject matter of jokes, identifying the material disguised by the joke-work (except in "innocent" jokes) as either hostile or obscene.[15] Yet, almost all human actions may be seen to have their source in these motives, which are, after all, at the center of our instinctual life. It may be argued that this subject matter, while still disguised, is closer to the surface, more obvious in events which make us laugh. In that case, however, we are no longer defining the ludicrous by content, but by the manner in which the content is presented, obviously or obliquely.

Indeed, in Freud's theory, content alone cannot by itself account for the laughter, because his view requires that part of our mind must respond to the aggressive or sexual content as if it were to be taken not comically, but seriously. He then imagines that energies in the service of conscience and repression are marshalled to repress our pleasure in this aggressive or sexual content. However, when we realize that we are in the presence of a joke, part of our energy which would have gone towards the full repression of our response, had the matter actually been serious, is now saved and expended in laughter. If his theory requires that the content of a joke must in one sense be taken seriously, then for Freud the distinguishing feature of a ludicrous incongruity is not any inherent ludicrousness in its content, but its joking style, which triggers our economizing on repressive energy. His first thesis "asserted that the characteristic of jokes lay in their form of expression."[16] Thus, except for his dramatic discovery of the psychological mechanisms that govern the relationships between our conscious and unconscious thought processes, his theory of ludicrousness is basically stylistic, and on the mechanism of stylistic process he does not have a great deal that is new to contribute. He understands that in ludicrous incongruity there is some transaction that occurs between the poles and that this process must occur with some suddenness or surprise. But this is not a major or an original contribution to the stylistic theory which presumes that any content can be made ludicrous by being presented in a ludicrous manner.

Almost all theories of style depend upon seeing incongruity as an element of a ludicrous style. It should be clear, however, from my earlier analysis, that while incongruity can be an element of style in general, there is no distinguishing difference between the way in which incongruity is employed in ludicrous and nonludicrous examples. Critics who sense this difficulty and aim at a more precise definition add a modifier such as surprising or sudden to specify ludicrous incongruity. But neither suddenness itself, nor suddenness of incongruity, generally causes laughter. Indeed, perfectly serious poetic incongruities reach our brain with the same speed as ludicrous ones, and yet they do not cause laughter. In fact, we can be made to laugh when an incongruity is drawn out with remarkable slowness. Or perhaps the crucial stylistic factor, as Herbert Spencer suggested, is the direction in which the meaning flows through the incongruity—downward, as he claims, for ludicrous incongruities, such as when one pole contains a high meaning that is deflated or reduced by the lower meaning of the other pole.[17] But we also laugh at incongruities that flow uphill. We laugh at a grownup wearing a child's too-tight shorts and propeller-driven beanie, and we laugh at the boy wearing his father's top hat and evening clothes. We can, given the proper context, be made to laugh at anything, and the means by which our laughter is provoked are probably as many and as various as there are stylistic devices themselves. In short, it has been and it may forever be impossible to identify any special ludicrous content or any special ludicrous style that exclusively defines ludicrous incongruity.

We may want to throw up our hands trying to explain this phenomenon. It is so singular in its effect, laughter, and yet so various in its causes that it would seem utterly to defy exact definition. But the approach I now propose clarifies and defines the nature of ludicrous incongruity. I will examine not style, not content, avenues which have proved unproductive, but another concept—context.

CHAPTER TWO

The Context of Comedy

I OFFER THIS definition: laughter results from an incongruity presented in a ludicrous context. That is, an incongruity, if it is to cause laughter, must be accompanied or preceded by a sufficient number of cues that indicate to an audience the risible intention of the incongruity and prepare them for the appropriate response of laughter.[1]

Advertisements announce that a certain theatrical performance is a comedy that provokes split sides and a laugh a minute. Television shows are provided with sound tracks of laughter lest the home viewer be confused about the appropriate response. Audiences go out to see nightclub comedians, not nightclub tragedians. Almost all comedic experiences require some form of cueing; certainly they run more smoothly to their laughing conclusion when such cues are present. Virtually all examples of artful ludicrous incongruity succeed precisely because the nature of the work is known in advance. Indeed, I would say that our laughter depends upon a ludicrous context which cues us to the nature of the experience we are about to enjoy and prepares us to receive it and react to it in a responsive manner.

Of course, the examples I have given so far have quite obvious cueing contexts. Let us consider for a moment the ambiguity that can occur when no apparent cueing exists, as when someone says something that may or may not be taken in a ludicrous light. How can we tell whether this incongruity is meant to be funny or serious? In our uncertainty we may ask the speaker, "Are you being funny?" or, as children often ask, "Funny ha ha, or funny strange?" The question completely stated is as follows: if the incongruity I have just perceived is not just a slip or some other unconscious construction, but is in fact intended, does it have a limited serious significance which you mean me to discover, or have I the freedom to discover whatever significance I can that makes me laugh? We feel secure about laughing when we know that we were intended to laugh at something and that everyone else is laughing too. On the other hand, we feel uncomfortable when we find ourselves laughing when no one else is, or when we discover upon second thought that our having laughed may have been inappropriate. The cueing context puts us on alert for the kind of response that is expected of us, alerts us to prepare the humorous frame of mind and mood necessary to receive ludicrous incongruities, and condones the wider range and depth of association and the more idiosyncratic significances that characterize our mental process in dealing with a ludicrous as opposed to a serious incongruity.

It should go without saying that we tend to laugh more when we are in a humorous frame of mind. Indeed, once we begin laughing at a series of ludicrous incongruities we may be made to laugh at anything. It is said that a successful comedian who has his audience rolling with laughter can read the telephone directory with humorous effect. I suppose that in a certain frame of mind, the fact that complete strangers are ranged together merely because of an adventitious significance given to the letters of their names can cause laughter. In fact, we will pay money to be entertained in this way; we will look forward to the pleasure and we will prepare our minds to receive it. On the other hand, if we are very much not in a humorous frame of mind, or if we are the sort of serious person who never laughs at anything, there is little that the humorist or comedian can do to make us laugh. We must prepare our minds for the humorous experience, or at least be open to the possibility of its working upon us. But this preparation or at least receptiveness is not much different in any other aesthetic experience. If we grudgingly go to the opera, then we are not likely to enjoy the experience. When we are presented with an incongruity without preparatory or contextual cueing, we sometimes are in doubt whether to take it seriously or humorously.

The cueing of the ludicrous context alerts us to be ready to receive the incongruity with the widest possible latitude of association and permit the most idiosyncratic linkages or significances to be discovered between the associations polarized by the incongruity. Moreover, it at the same time justifies and condones our laughing reaction—a response which is normally hedged by social, religious, political, and psychological restrictions. When we are in doubt about the nature and intention of an incongruity, we are more inclined to play safe and take it seriously; that is, we tend to narrow the latitude of associations and to consider only the more meaningful or reasonable linkages or significances between the associations polarized by the incongruity. Thus, an incongruity that might have made us laugh had it been given a clear ludicrous context is instead treated seriously, or very likely seriously, when given an ambiguous context and when we are not in a ludicrous mood to begin with.

In elevating the importance of the idea of context, I reject those interpretations that favor content and style for the reasons I have already given. However, to some readers, it may at first appear that context and style are so close as not to be worth the fuss of discriminating between them or of adding yet another term to a subject already confused with an extensive and imprecise terminology. To be sure, a ludicrous context, while it is frequently established by such a simple device as mere assertion—"Did you hear this joke?"—may also be indicated by a wide variety of stylistic cues. But the difficulty and the point is that no one stylistic device, or even any collection of such devices, appears to be crucial in effecting a laughing response to an incongruity. "Ludicrous context" would be a more dependable addition to the critical terminology concerning laughter were it possible to say in advance what particular form it will take, were it possible, for example, to provide a clear formula or recipe for it. While we cannot in such a protean subject hope for that degree of certitude, we are able, after a successful episode of ludicrousness, to analyze what factors contributed to the establishment and maintenance of that particular successful ludicrous context.

I will now discuss a characteristic alluded to earlier, the irrational or extremely idiosyncratic nature of the significances or linkages discovered between the trains of association arising out of incongruities presented in a ludicrous, as opposed to a serious, context. What the ludicrous context does is to suggest that for the purpose of pleasure, and during the extent of the ludicrous event, we may allow ourselves to suspend the rules by which we normally live—the laws of nature, the restrictions of morality, the sequences of logical thought, the demands of rationality–in short, we are encouraged to suspend the internal law of gravity, our seriousness. We are asked to find in the matter presented to us whatever gives us the pleasure that expresses itself in laughter, and we are also given a general pardon and indulgence against whatever breaches of logic, decorum, and morality we may make in arriving at that pleasure.

In the ludicrous context, pleasure is all. The dramatist, the poet, the novelist may wish to ask his admirers whether they not only enjoyed but understood his work. The humorist or comedian is satisfied, indeed he must be satisfied only with the audience's laughter. We are not required to understand the actual content of our laughter. The context encourages this uncritical response and implicitly guards us against outside prying and even self-analysis. For the context asks only that we laugh, not that we all laugh at the same idea. The actual triggering idea for one person's laughter may be radically different from another's, and yet this discrepancy, in practical effect, matters not a whit. We are hardly ever called to account for our laughter, and if we are, we usually reply simply that we laughed because the thing was funny, and unless the questioner is our psychiatrist, or a literary critic, or our public school teacher, that answer generally suffices.

One of the reasons why laughter is so well defended against inquiry is that it is essentially a private pleasure. But it is a private pleasure which, because of the fact of its vocalization, becomes a public expression. Therefore, the secrecy of motive, even from ourselves, is of great service. Think of how we would have to defend ourselves if, for example, every time we experienced a sexual feeling, we sneezed out loud and everyone knew exactly what the sneezing meant. With laughter, everyone in a way does sense how potentially objectionable the triggering idea is, but agrees not to recognize or discuss it. There develops a conspiracy of ignorance and silence. We agree not to inquire into each other's reasons or even into our own personal reasons for laughter. The ludicrous context is built of these sound-proof panels, a safe room where pleasure may be obtained with no one, especially ourselves, the wiser. Thus the ludicrous context provides us with a convenient explanation and a justification for our public display of an essentially private and secret source of pleasure.

The context of the ludicrous is the private world of pleasure for its own sake. It is a holiday from the economic transactions with reality that reason usually negotiates. Some students of this phenomenon strive to find a functional aspect in it. Sociologists may see in the scornful element in laughter a purpose that reinforces group stand-ards and ventilates social hostility;[2] some students of learning de-velopment and communication see it as a learned response, a means by which the young child assures his parents of his wellbeing before he acquires the capacity for speech.[3] But the impression remains that none of these purposes, nor even all of them combined, satisfactorily accounts for the development of this capacity for laughter. I think that it is therefore best to regard it in the way it is commonly ac-cepted—as a source of pleasure that is distinctly human. All of our instincts are in the service of survival. But in laughter we experience an explosion of pleasure, a vocal and conspicuous display of delight that in effect incapacitates us, while it lasts, for any other business. This is an indulgence apparently granted no other creature. Perhaps we alone have mastered reality just enough so that we feel we have a surplus of physical and mental energy that can be expended for the sake of imaginary pleasure alone.

Essential to the ludicrous context is the principle that nothing is relevant except the laughter which it is designed to encourage. The ludicrous context is established to allow us to suspend for the moment and for the purpose of laughter any and all considerations that might interfere with this pleasure. Of course, the larger context in which a particular ludicrous incongruity occurs (for example, an epic poem, a tragedy, or an otherwise serious novel), may encourage us to dis-cover meaningful significances, etc. The point I am making is that within the narrower, specific ludicrous context that allows laughter there can be nothing that distracts from that particular intention. The context serves this pleasure, makes us anticipate it, cues us to search within ourselves for the private triggering mechanisms that produce it, and finally condones our pleasure in it.

While it is true that the mental process by which the mind solves incongruities is exactly the same whether the incongruities are lu-dicrous or serious, the purpose, or the intention, is radically different. In serious examples, we put ourselves in the mood to explore only strongly meaningful or relevant linkages or significances that join the trains of association emanating from the poles of the incongruity. The significance that we discover and the pleasure that we feel engage us with reality. But the ludicrous context works towards an opposite purpose. It suggests that we explore the trains of association not in search of truth, but pleasure. If to the discovery of truth pleasure may, some say must, attach, it is also true that the enjoyment of pleasure may occur without any significant attachment of truth. And the ludicrous context encourages and condones this quest for pleasure without serious or significant meaning.

The ludicrous context informs you that within its purview is an incongruity with which you may do what you will so long as what you make of it gives you the pleasure of laughter. It tells you that you may, indeed that you *must* give full freedom to your process of thought. You must be bound by no restriction of relevancy or morality. In this special sense, I term laughter irrelevant. It is a vacation from the workaday economy of the mind by which the pleasure of meaning and significance is purchased by the effort of mental work. But the humorous context says, enjoy! Get the most pleasure from the least amount of effort. Don't sift through the serious significances and linkages. Don't trouble with weighing them, judging them. Use no judgment at all! *Any* significance, *any* linkage whatsoever will do—the first one that is funny enough to make you laugh. It is as if our mental banker went berserk and began giving out souvenirs. The ludicrous context and the mental process it encourages are a mockery of the whole costly process by which we experience and interpret reality and pay for our knowledge and mastery. In our experience of the ludicrous context our mental economy is turned topsy-turvy. We invest little and enjoy huge returns. And moreover, we are encouraged to feel no guilt for our killing, because the humorous context tells us that it was all a joke. None of it is to be taken seriously.

How do we come to this pleasure? I do not think that it is possible to categorize all of the stylistic devices and cueing mechanisms that belong to the ludicrous context. A device might be as simple as a blatant cue: "Here is a joke." Or it could be as delicate as a subtle nuance of tone. While it appears impossible to generalize about the various cueing mechanisms that define the ludicrous context, we can in broad terms discuss their effect, which is to prepare our mind for the pleasurable irrelevancies that characterize the outcome of our mental work upon incongruities in a ludicrous context. There is no difference here in the means by which we are made to anticipate a comic event or a lyric poem. We select a particular kind of work, anticipating the sort of experience and pleasure that kind of art is known to supply. Even in advance of the actual experience of it, we adjust our mind and mood to receive it most effectively. Although our minds and moods are not entirely within our power to manipulate, they are enough so, or often enough so, that this faculty of anticipation plays an important role in our aesthetic experience in general, and in our experience of artful ludicrousness in particular. Had we not this faculty, we could not return to the composition of a courteous letter after an annoying interruption on the telephone. If this faculty did not exist, we would not have novels, only short stories written in great speed at one sitting while and only as long as the artist's mood lasted.

It is evident that we do possess a limited power to will our mood and to organize in a very broad way, to be sure, the images in our mind, both conscious and unconscious, that normally attach to that particular mood. Without such a capacity, we could not explain the unity that occurs in matters great and small, conscious and unconscious, in successful works of art. There can be no doubt that the capacity to recall a mood and to return with accuracy to it with all of the images, conscious as well as unconscious, that are normally associated with it, is one of the special distinctions of the artistic personality. But surely, this same capacity, if in lesser degree, exists as a potentiality in us all, and plays a significant role in our aesthetic experience. And it exerts, in my view, a particularly crucial influence upon our experience of ludicrous incongruity as distinct from all other artful forms of incongruity, for the ludicrous variety offers wider ranges of idiosyncratic or irrelevant signification. In other forms, while anticipation speeds as well as intensifies our appropriate response to it, there is in the content enough relevant, significant meaning so that we may work our way towards an appropriate reaction. But laughter is never sprung by ratiocination.

If the context and anticipation are helpful to all forms of artistic experience, they are essential to the ludicrous. While other forms of art contain within themselves the means to lead us towards a state of mind and mood appropriate to them, laughter in the first place utterly depends upon our already being in a humorous frame of mind and mood. In this respect, the ludicrous context, however slippery it may be and resistant to exact characterization, because it functions

as the prerequisite of laughter, stands as a central idea in any definition of ludicrous incongruity. It is as important an idea as incongruity itself. So much so that, in the definition I offer, the word
ludicrous does not modify incongruity at all since, as I have shown,
there is nothing laughable in either the nature or the content of incongruity. My definition reads as follows: laughter is the result of an
incongruity in a ludicrous context.

The concept of the ludicrous context can and ought to be applied
to individual works of the comic spirit. I shall make attempts in that
direction in later chapters. At this time I would observe that while
I cannot provide a recipe of devices for the generation of the ludicrous
context within a work of art, I can generally discuss the mental effects
of those devices within the reader's own mental context of laughter.
This inner context in the reader may be seen as a locus in the mind,
a mental mood-place like any other such mood-place, the lyric or the
tragic, to which he has some power to repair given the proper cues
and incentives and barring any stronger mental and emotional claims.
Thus we may say, "Tickle me"; or we may say, "Do not bother me
now with your jokes. I have other things to think about." The mental
context of laughter, I feel, is best viewed as such a place in the mind,
and while I do not think it possible to categorize all the paths and
conveyances by which we can be brought to this place, I do believe
I can describe something of the nature of the place itself.

I will adduce to the mental context of laughter three salient features.
It is a place of mental pleasure without the mediation of reason,
without the expenditure of work, and without the censorship of morality. An incongruity, as I have shown, when presented in a ludicrous context, does not require a reasonable significance as a solution.
Were the opposite the case, laughter would be more common among
philosophers than school children. In fact, there is no requirement
that the significance discovered share any common interest with the
rules of logic, with the limitations of the internal associative process
we usually regard in ourselves as normal, or with the organization
and distribution of external matter and energy that we normally term
reality. To agree to this proposition is to agree also that, in a sense,
laughter signals a mental and emotional process that extracts pleasure
from irrelevancy. Given the same incongruity, the reasonable man
in a serious frame of mind extracts meaning or concludes that there

is nothing of moment present, while the man in a humorous frame of mind extracts from the same incongruity not necessarily meaning but the pleasure signified by laughter.

The mental process of pleasure which is expressed in laughter finds no increase or advantage from its coincidence with the mental process we call reason and by which we apprehend the world we normally call reality. In this sense, the process that produces laughter is irrational and based upon irrelevancy. I do not mean that the process yields no significance whatsoever. For incongruity must be defined as a discrepancy or a polarity which, however wide, must still contain some, however slender linkage or significance. My point is that an incongruity, when presented in a ludicrous context, must yield, if it is to achieve its effect, some sort of linkage between its parts, but the significance that satisfies the requirement of this incongruity is unbounded by the limitations of rationality and reality. This is not to say that in the mental process that precedes laughter our sense of reason and reality lies dormant, but only that there is no reward in its exercise. Rather, our energy turns toward solutions that are irrelevant, idiosyncratic, irrational, pseudorational. We do not lose our minds, but the ludicrous context does allow us to enjoy, for a time, and if we will, the pleasure of mental processes that are normally dysfunctional and proscribed by our practical investment in the process of reason and in the world of reality that process seeks to interpret to our practical advantage.

Laughter is an utterly self-absorbing process, utterly irresponsible and for its own sake. Were the process of laughter not so completely devoted to pleasure, we might characterize it as involving work. If work is understood as a transaction by which a certain amount of energy is exchanged for a practical advantage or result, the mental process that yields or aims to yield a useful significance may be said to involve work, but the same cannot be said of the mental process that yields laughter. It is a process still more extreme than play, but closer to play than to work. The mental locus of laughter and that of play share some features, the main one being that both establish a fantasy world devoted to the enjoyment of pleasure. But the difference between them, and it is a difference which removes laughter further from the principle of work, is that while the interest in play is pleasure, its effect is to prepare the player for the real world.[4] Play is profitably viewed as a field of pleasurable practice upon which are exercised, learned, and perfected those skills which will be of practical advantage in the real world. In this sense, the mental context of play is much closer to the serious mind-state of work than is the mental context of laughter. Laughter, alone, is for the indulgence of pleasure.

To make another distinction, witticisms often fail to stimulate actual laughter because while they contain an incongruity, the context may not entirely exclude rationality and work. Too often, the witty remark, instead of allowing the easiest and least rational solution to the offered incongruity, rather demands and rewards work and conscious thought. It is generally the nature of wit to have too much point to produce laughter. Wit has, by comparison, a fairly limited range of meaning, as in Dr. Johnson's witty definition: "A fishing rod is a stick with a hook at one end and a fool at the other"; or in Mencken's definition of love as "the delusion that one woman differs from another."[5] Similarly, humorous riddles tend not to inspire actual laughter in adults. "What has four legs and flies?" Adults, unlike children, tend to treat the question as a serious challenge, requiring real thought and work. What *does* have four legs and flies? Children more easily enter into the convention and enjoy the nonsense of the answer—"A dead horse!"—with its implicit parody and criticism of adult logic.[6] Any serious appeal which arouses our rational faculties or which promises a practical workaday reward can puncture the ludicrous context.

The pleasure of laughter seems not to be bought and paid for at the same rate of exchange that we normally use to buy and pay for other pleasures. Suddenly, the mind becomes a generous marketplace in which unaccountably we get more for less. This mystery deserves understanding. It is as if we went around the corner to a discount store where our pleasures cost us less. And in a sense, this analogy is quite appropriate. The ludicrous context cues us to move mentally around the corner to that mood-place, the locus of the ludicrous context in the mind where, indeed, our pleasures do cost less. There are other states of the mind where the economy is intensely more rigorous, where in more serious matters we purchase, for example, the pleasure associated with Mozart or with mathematical problem-solving at much greater cost. These are not laughing matters. And that is precisely the point.

In serious as opposed to ludicrous problem-solving, the answers have at least a relative and ideally an absolute correlation to reality. We are not, or ought not to be, satisfied with answers that only seem responsive or are only partially responsive to the question. In serious matters we feel, or ought to feel, obliged to test the answer in the real world or by means of competition with other potentially correct answers. We may not accept just *any* answer. That is, serious significances compete in an economic market of meanings wherein some of them earn credibility, more or less, according to the value we place upon them. But in ludicrous significances, we have no responsibility to anything except our desire for the pleasure of laughter. The context places upon us no obligation to discover profound, true, or in any way valuable significances. We are not obliged to test first significances arrived at spontaneously against others reached later upon reflection. If the first one makes us laugh, it is enough—we are satisfied. That is, in the mental context of ludicrousness, the process that yields laughter need not find the *best* reason to laugh, only the *first sufficient reason*.

I do not think it meaningful to apply the term work to such a mental process that yields so large an effect from so slender an effort, and an effort that is so little, indeed, I believe not at all bound by the restrictions that usually define and give value to the product of effort. Moreover, the infinite variety, the idiosyncrasy, the very irrationality of the paths that lead to the uniform result of laughter make it difficult to term as work the energy expended to reach that result. In my view, it is theoretically possible for an audience to laugh at a particular joke for as many reasons and by as many different routes as there are individuals in that audience. Yet give that same audience a column of figures to sum, and they will set about adding them up in one of only a very few ways, and if they have made no mistake in their work, they will arrive at the same result. But there is no similarity between this effort and its uniform result, and the incomparably various process of personal signification, the incomparably various personal reasons for which each member of an audience contributes his voice to the uniform result of laughter. Ask an individual to show you how he did his addition, and he will teach you his method. But you will get no sense from the laughing member of the audience if you ask him how he came to be laughing. The fact is, he truly does not know. The process is so swift and so unconscious that its exact mechanism is beyond explanation. It is only the effect, the laughter, that is important. It is all for pleasure, and the first way to it is the one that is taken.

Equally significant for the functioning of the ludicrous context is its freedom from moral restraint. The fact that comedy and morality are mutually antagonistic cannot go unnoticed. Later I will explore the striking example of Lenny Bruce's comedy. We know that a great many jokes and occasions for laughter arise through a subversion of the rules of morality. Indeed, Freud thought that all laughter at jokes arises from the sheer pleasure of subverting the rules of morality.[7] But Freud left unclear the reason why the all-powerful, all-seeing superego would tolerate such an affront, however devious, within its domain. How can it be, as the psychoanalyst Edmund Bergler asked, that the superego, in Freud's own terms a cruel, omniscient taskmaster, is so easily duped by any stock comedian?[8] Freud, a Victorian after all, saw comedy as sneaking a modicum of repressive energy for the purpose of pleasure while the psychical forces favoring morality and immorality were preoccupied in debate. Laughter is seen as the result of a tactical victory of wit in the service of immorality against conscience. The theory depends upon duplicity, and yet the success of the duplicity cannot be practically explained.

These problems become different, and, as we shall see, more susceptible to consistent and complete analysis if we understand laughter not in terms of immorality, but amorality. That is to say, the mental operations that yield ludicrous significance take place in an atmosphere into which moral concerns temporarily, at least, are constrained from interfering. There is, in effect, a context of the mind, a mood-place that corresponds to the external context for ludicrous incongruities, which is uniquely characterized by its freedom from morality, just as it is also characterized by its freedom from relevancy and work. The uniqueness of this mental context is that all of our moral, practical, and rational concerns that normally limit our pleasure are still present, but as long as we remain mentally in that mood-place, we effect a moratorium on their functioning. They are present, but they have not their wonted force or effect. They are present merely and only for the purpose of our pleasure in laughter, and we may use them for this purpose as long as and until our pleasure has been served or until for other reasons we leave this privileged context. Charles Lamb, in describing his pleasure in Restoration dramatic comedy, drew the topography of the ludicrous context in a wonderful way:

> I am glad for a season to take an airing beyond the diocese of the strict conscience—not to live always in the precincts of the law-courts,—but now and then, for a dream-while or so, to imagine a world with no meddling restrictions—to get into recesses, whither the hunter cannot follow me—
> . . . Secret shades
> Of woody Ida's inmost grove,
> While yet there was no fear of Jove.
> I come back to my cage and my restraint the fresher and more healthy for it. I wear my shackles more contentedly for having respired the breath of an imaginary freedom. I do not know how it is with others, but I feel the better always for the perusal of one of Congreve's—nay, why should I not add even of Wycherley's—comedies. I am the gayer at least for it; and I could never connect those sports of a witty fancy in any shape with any result to be drawn from them to imitation of real life. They are a world of themselves almost as much as fairyland. . . . It is altogether a speculative scene of things, which has no reference whatever to the world that is.[9]

What Lamb says of Restoration comedy, I would enlarge to include the entire mental context of ludicrousness. It is a privileged context unlike any other in the mind. Here all factors are present without their usual effects, for they are present not to make sense of, to regulate, or to use our response to the incongruity introduced there. There is, in short, at the moment of laughter, a willing suspension of all normal mental process. What I am saying is that laughter is not profitably viewed as one of many various but essentially similar mental transactions, but rather as a unique event, more different from than similar to what we would term normal mental process. It is as if the whole mind shifts into another gear. It involves a special state of mind, a special state of consciousness.

It may well be asked why the superego in the first place tolerates the establishment of this privileged state of mind. One attraction of looking at the problem in this contextual rather than psychoanalytic way is its simplicity. It is much more economical to imagine a whole state of mind accorded special privileges than to attempt to explain

the precise mechanisms by which each individual joke earns its separate and forged credentials for bypassing morality. It is not as if, for
example, reason and work are utterly subverted in this state of ludicrous consciousness. If, heaven forbid, smoke billowed into the
auditorium, no matter how funny the comedian was, reason would
spring into action to interrupt the happy state of mind. Is the smoke
part of the act? If not, where is the nearest exit? Reason and soon the
whole body would begin to work in earnest. So too is morality in the
ludicrous context shifted into a state of suspended readiness. It is
not, any more than reason and work were not, banished utterly from
the ludicrous context. They all must be present, for laughter is generally sprung by making one or more of them the butts of the joke.
They are present for the sake of laughter. So the question really is,
why do they permit this use to be made of them? And the answer
is that we would have it so.

Our states of mind, as I have argued earlier, are to some degree
within our power to will into being. From the contextual point of
view, it is not that the superego, for example, ceases to function; in
the amoral context of ludicrousness, its functions are happily tinted
by the willingness to laugh. We may view morality as rhetorically
giving the usual literal messages; only the tone is changed by the
new context. But we know when our moral voice really means what
it says. We know when we really, seriously are endangered. We
know the difference between art and reality. Sir Philip Sidney stated
it in this way: "What child is there that, coming to a play, and seeing
Thebes written in great letters upon an old door, doth believe that
it is Thebes?" [10] We permit the establishment of the ludicrous context
precisely because we wish the pleasure of laughter and because we
know, indeed, we are confident that were any real threat to manifest
itself, our sense of reason and morality would recall us to the serious
work at hand. Our superego is flattered by our faith in its authority.
It is, in fact, our supreme confidence in the authority of the rule of
our sense of morality, our reason, and our instinct for survival that
permits us to take these vacations into the luxury of fantasy pleasures.

My view of the cueing context is most directly challenged by the
existence of natural ludicrous incongruity, that is, an incongruity
causing laughter that appears contrived by no one or nothing but
chance. The challenge arises because there appears to be no context

for natural incongruity. If the context, in demanding and condoning laughter, is a useful idea, how then is natural laughter to be explained? Why do we laugh, barring complicating factors, when someone at a cocktail party coughs and spews his drink on those around him? An example like this could force us back to theories we earlier rejected: for example, that some things in nature are inherently ludicrous, spewing, in this case; or that there is a special kind of incongruity which is inherently ludicrous. But the theories examined earlier had only a limited usefulness. They functioned with one kind of situation that provokes laughter, but they failed with others. By the introduction of the idea of a ludicrous context with its ability to provoke a parallel mental state of ludicrousness, I am aiming at a general theory that will serve the entire range of situations that raise laughter.

I will therefore attempt to carry the idea of a ludicrous context into the analysis of natural laughter, which only at first seems to be accompanied by no context at all. The function of the context in artificial ludicrous incongruities is first to identify, then facilitate, and finally condone laughable matter. A ludicrous incongruity in nature, by contrast, labors under a disadvantage in evoking its laughing response. Far from being a simpler matter, an incongruity in nature that causes laughter requires of its audience many more and more complex mental operations than does the same incongruity within a contrived and clear ludicrous context. Natural, here, does not mean simple. Art, here as in other cases, is a clarification of nature in the service of reliable pleasure.

Above, when I mentioned the example of natural ludicrous incongruity—a grown person at one moment consuming his drink properly and at the next spewing it upon his social partners—I stipulated the condition that laughter would result, *barring complicating factors*. This is an important condition for laughter because in a natural ludicrous incongruity there are *always* complicating factors. The salient virtue of the ludicrous context in artful comedy is precisely that it does bar or at least aims to bar these complicating factors. The artist seeks to present an incongruity not within the complex and ambiguous context of reality and nature, but within a specifically limited ludicrous context from which he purposefully bars all factors that might inhibit or preclude laughter. Among these factors inimical to laughter may be included the audience's potential to sympathize with or identify too closely with the embarrassment or even the actual physical pain of the butt of the jest; the audience's potential for moral judgment which may be unfortunately activated by the content of the incongruity; the audience's potential for treating the incongruity in a realistic or relevant way, as one requiring a relevant and realistic solution rather than any solution that produces laughter; in short, the audience's potential to be the opposite of humorous, dead serious. With all the impediments against which natural incongruities labor, it is more wonder that people nevertheless find reasons to laugh at them at all.

While in one light incongruities in nature that cause laughter are literally fortuitous, in another light we may view them as having an implicit intention. After all, it is not general nature or reality that has an interest in joining two objects in an incongruity that incidentally causes laughter in humans. The objects each pursue their separate interests, the least of which is to act the comedian for the passing pleasure of human beings. The motive that urges a dog to defecate next to the politician's soap box is comedic or satiric neither in the dog's mind nor in that of the windy speech-maker. But the audience's laughter does indicate that they have agreed to impose a kind of ludicrous context upon this otherwise neutral juxtaposition.

Especially with natural ludicrous incongruity, the ludicrousness is in the mind of the laugher. As with the artful variety, laughter is not the result of any naturally risible object within the incongruity, nor of the fact of incongruity itself, nor of any special style or kind—a ludicrous kind—of incongruity. Rather, it is the result of a willingness, sometimes a willfulness, to view the natural incongruity in a ludicrous as opposed to any other context. With artful ludicrous incongruity the audience is upon surer footing, relying upon the information, especially the emotional cues, conveyed by the more or less obvious context. But with the natural variety, we each become our own comic artist: we each establish our own ludicrous context and find within it our own joke. So there is, after all, an author even of natural ludicrous incongruity. It is ourselves.

However, in this act of comedic creation, we become bound by the increased responsibilities of authorship. It is much simpler for us to be a passive audience presented with a patently ludicrous context that encourages and condones laughter. But when we see an incongruity in nature that might cause laughter, we are left on our own to determine instantaneously whether that response would be appropriate in the neutral context that surrounds the incongruity. This is by no means a simple determination, as experience will confirm when in a group we alone laughed, or alone remained serious while the others laughed. When we are presented with a natural incongruity, our primary decision is to determine whether it affects us in a ludicrous or a serious way. This is an important decision because one would guess that the vast majority of incongruities in nature offer real problems that demand serious consideration and relevant solutions. Except in the artfully ludicrous context of the circus, it does not pay to laugh at a bear with a beanie on its head.

Natural incongruities generally contain significances that concern and interest us in a serious way. So the first and probably the most important question the viewer of a natural incongruity must ask himself is, how seriously does this incongruity involve me? How much, or at all, for example, does this natural incongruity present any threat to my survival, or to matters I hold valuable, such as my family, my friends, my morals, my country, my money, etc.? Although we can be encouraged to laugh at these matters when they are presented in an obviously artful ludicrous context, we have a difficult decision when they present themselves naturally and ambiguously within the neutral context of reality. It is true that there are bizarre examples, such as condemned men finding something laughable on the way to execution. But these are extreme cases that prove that we do have some power willfully to distance ourselves from reality and that we must experience this distance or else exercise our power to achieve it before we can laugh at an incongruity in nature. In effect, we do the comedian's work by barring complicating factors and isolating the incongruity within a private ludicrous context.

We have reached an important conclusion about the importance of the concept of the ludicrous context. It is, in short, the essential prerequisite to laughter, since any incongruity can be made laughable in a ludicrous context, and no incongruity, not even those occuring in nature, can be made laughable without it. The special value of this concept is that it identifies an essential condition for laughter which has parallel aesthetic and psychological implications, identifying factors that must exist both in the work and in the state of mind of the laughter. My intention now is to study in practical examples some, though by no means all, of the characteristics of the ludicrous context.

CHAPTER THREE

Jokes

ART IS a means of repeating, improving upon, and rendering reliable the pleasures of the imagination that occur spontaneously in reality. Jokes share in the advantages that belong to art in general. A joke, as we hear it delivered by a comedian on television, or in a nightclub performance, or retold by a friend, is hardly ever a spontaneous creation. It had been prepared in advance for professional performance, or it had been heard before and at a particular time recalled and retold for the amusement of a friend. This is not to say that the conversation of comedians and of our humorous friends is not funny—only that their spontaneous creations are to be understood as witticisms, or as joking, not necessarily as true jokes. This is a difference worth observing—the difference between being funny and being an artist, that is to say, the difference between the comedy of everyday life and the art of comedy.

Every day supplies ample material for the amateur humorist. Each day spontaneously offers incongruous natural events upon which he may impose a ludicrous context, or else he may create his own opportunities to join incongruities within a ludicrous context. At times we play the amateur comedian, at others we become his informally gathered audience. The give-and-take of this kind of commonplace laughter is so natural, so much a part of the common emotional experience of everyday life that we take it for granted and do not notice it as a remarkable occurrence, unless, of course, one of our comrades happens to be an obsessively funny person who keeps us always in stitches, or unless, indeed, we are such a person ourselves. Being funny at this amateur level rarely entails making, or even telling, true jokes. What it does involve is the spontaneous isolation of incongruities within a ludicrous context. My point is that no matter how successful this enterprise is at the time, no matter how much we make others laugh, or are made to laugh ourselves, the episode can hardly ever be recreated later in precisely the same way. When we do try to reachieve it, we almost always fail. "I guess you had to be there," is our lame excuse. But it is an excuse that supports my argument that essential to laughter is the concept of a ludicrous context, a place, and especially a mental place or state of mind in which laughter can occur.

The trouble with the commonplace laughter of everyday life is that the incongruous materials and the ludicrous context which support the laughter are highly transitory and difficult if not generally impossible to reassemble. Someone says something and we reply and there is laughter at the repartee. Or we see something and we say something and there is laughter at the observation. At that time, and within the ludicrous context of that time, these observations and repartees were funny, but only a short while later we may not be able even to recall what we had said, or if we were able to remember, we probably would not be able precisely to reconstruct the same ludicrous context. "I guess you just had to be there." If, for example, I wanted to share with you a really amusing thing that happened yesterday, I would first have to tell you that it occurred while I was talking with Harold Grayson who is that very short man in the biology department. Well, he had been out for some minor surgery and when he got back, the department secretary, you know the one I mean—you don't?—I think her name is Karen. It's important because you have to be able to picture her face. She was filling out his health forms. . . . Enough of this. This kind of story demands a good raconteur, and even then you might still have to know Karen, if that really is her name. And yet were the story indeed successfully told, it still would not be a true joke.

The ludicrous context that is established around commonplace laughable events and observations is comparatively more delicate than the one that obtains in true jokes. For the ludicrous context which is generated extemporaneously very much depends upon a shared understanding of relatively intimate facts, nuances, and gestures. In the above example, if you do happen to know Karen and the sort of face she is capable of making under certain circumstances, then you are in a privileged position to enter into this particular ludicrous context and enjoy the pleasure of this particular moment of laughter. It is, I repeat, extremely difficult, if not impossible, exactly to recreate these commonplace ludicrous events. The incongruity may be recognizable only to those who see it at that moment, and the ludicrous context itself may subsist upon such subtleties of tone, gesture, and privileged knowledge as to be beyond accurate repetition. In short, the particular incongruities and their ludicrous context which cause the commonplace laughter in our everyday lives could not possibly become, verbatim, the jokes of a professional comedian. The professional has countless jokes about mothers-in-law, traffic jams, tax collectors, drunkards, but how many times a day do we ourselves find incongruities in these subjects and establish them within a ludicrous context? There can be no doubt but that everyday life provides the material for the comedian's jokes, but it is also true that jokes are categorically different from all of the witticisms, repartees, observations, and events that account for the vast majority of our daily laughter.

To be honest, we must admit that most of the things that evoke our daily laughter really are, by contrast to the best work of professional comedians, pretty insignificant. That is to say, they rarely bear repetition. Even when something happens or is said at which we are laughing our heartiest laugh and we say, "That's the funniest thing I ever saw," we know we will never be able faithfully to share it later with anyone who was not there when it happened. Why did you have to be there? In common practice, the ludicrous context is an extremely tenuous sphere of influence that is established and sustained by means of the most accidental and subtle cues. If you were, in fact, "there," that is, if you willingly shared in the complex set of verbal and nonverbal gestures that led to the presentation of the incongruity in the ludicrous context, then you laughed. Sometimes two people see something and they look into each other's eyes and burst out laughing. And if their other companions ask them what they are laughing about, the two may laugh even harder, or, if they try to explain, utterly fail. Even though the others were physically present, they were not mentally and emotionally "there," sharing in the ludicrous context that the other two had suddenly and silently established. At other times, the most trivial visual and verbal incongruities are sufficient to allow us the pleasure of laughter.

The more I think of the occasions of commonplace laughter, the more convinced I am of the value of the idea of the ludicrous context. For in everyday laughter, surely what is so funny is not simply the way that that man has parted his hair, or the really trivial quip that the beautiful secretary offered at the Christmas party, or the mere fact that our son has put his pants on backwards (we would not have laughed if the schoolbus were honking at our curb). Laughter does not derive from any specific content, or even from the fact of incongruity. The commonplace laughter of everyday life, more clearly than artful comedy, shows how essential to any definition is the idea of context, our willingness to laugh at even the most slender incongruities.

The professional comedian, however, cannot count on the kind of special relationship that we have with our son, or on the kind of affability and generosity we feel for beautiful secretaries, especially at Christmas time. He must do better. The comedian's jokes are an adaptation of commonplace humor towards generalization and reliability. Jokes must compete in the marketplace of pleasures associated with laughter, and for that reason their materials must be less privileged, less personally limited, and their ludicrous context must be wider than obtains in daily extemporaneous provocations to laughter. In short, jokes must be more efficient, more open to a wider variety of common experience and association than, say, extemporaneous witticisms and informal joking.

All laughter is the result of the apprehension of an incongruity within a ludicrous context which I have described as a state of mind from which rationality, morality, and work have been temporarily excluded. Jokes attempt to optimize all of these characteristics in a way that extemporaneous joking achieves rather by sudden intuition and familiar consent than by formal design.

One of the especially interesting aspects of jokes to the literary critic is that they create the comic experience in an extremely radical and economical form. In a very short scene, they must engender the ludicrous context, engage the audience's participation, and introduce in the briefest way those particular incongruities of plot, character, or thought that continue to support the ludicrous context and that permit the laughter which signals a successful conclusion.

With our broader understanding that the true shape of a joke extends beyond the narrow boundaries of the joke's words to include

the ludicrous context in which the words are set, we know that the
comedian must immediately by implicit or explicit means establish
the ludicrous context. Once that is accomplished, the joke begins:

> A Texan was visiting the Louvre . . .
> Two psychiatrists meet on a street corner . . .
> The little moron thinks that . . .
> A travelling salesman . . .
> His mother-in-law is so mean . . .
> A man came home early and found his wife in bed with another
> man . . .

The joke must begin in a way that will not disrupt the ludicrous
context, which I have characterized as lacking in morality, rationality,
and work. A Texan pays his visit, or a husband comes home early,
or a salesman experiences car trouble on a country road. These are
not real people, nor are their problems and embarrassments made
real to us. It is not even accurate to say that they are stereotypes, for
stereotypes at least contain some truth, albeit distorted. The ludicrous
context does not require that its contents have any more relevance
to reality than is strictly necessary to make apparent its main burden,
the incongruity that triggers our laughter.

The degree of relevancy for jokes is quite small. "A" Texan visits
the Louvre. His name is not required, and in general would prove
a distraction were it offered. "Mr. Joseph Hillman of Texas" visits the
Louvre. No. A joke is not a novel and requires no pretense of biographical verisimilitude. The joke makes this clear by introducing
"a" Texan; "a" newlywed couple; "a" travelling salesman; "these
three" nuns; "this" priest, "this" minister, and "this" rabbi. . . .
Now, while it is true that many jokes refer to actual persons, and
belong to that class of real or invented anecdote that accumulates
around the names of certain famous humorous personalities, these
are surely a special class of humor. True jokes may occasionally ben-
efit from the inclusion of famous names; they rarely find improvement
from apparently real but ordinary names. As a general rule, jokes
employ the least degree of verisimilitude and specificity required to
make the incongruity apparent.

When in a ludicrous context "a" Texan visits the Louvre, we look
forward to a punchline that makes us laugh rather than deals sen-

sitively or accurately with Texans or with the Louvre. If a certain number of jokes might be served by this introduction, it would be true that that number would be reduced somewhat by changing the introduction to "A man from Montana visits the Louvre," because Texas has a wider and richer field of association than has Montana. Now there may be much that can be said about a Texan's native state and France's famous museum that in an informative and useful way does justice to both. But that would take place in a different context. Judicious, objective truth does not fall within the purview of the ludicrous context.

The objects introduced into the ludicrous context ought to have the most general, even idiosyncratic reference possible. They are like convex mirrors which not only reflect the audience's first and direct ideas, but also distort these ideas, and moreover draw into sight a much wider than normal view of associated ideas which would otherwise lurk far beyond the periphery of awareness. And as this is so, the joke may be said to hold up a mirror to inner nature. But what do we see imaged there? At first, nothing but the most perfunctory surface mechanism of the joke itself. The personal response in all its complexity remains hidden and more guarded against discovery than the effect of any other kind of literature. I can only with the greatest difficulty barely discern hints of my own nature reflected in the joke's private mirror. And this is as it should be.

It is the nature both of the ludicrous context and of the allusive materials contained therein to foster in the audience the widest possible range of idiosyncratic signification. The incongruity present in poetic metaphor also encourages personal signification. We are not dealing in either case with facts, but with incongruities which inspire personal meaning. But the range of signification is far wider in jokes than in poetic metaphor, for our response to the latter is modified and narrowed by the serious context and by the influence of many other adjacent metaphoric centers of meaning. So that while a reader may wish to impose an idiosyncratic significance upon one poetic incongruity—everyone is entitled to one mistake—the other metaphors cooperate to resist such imposition. A joke, however, contains at least one incongruity but never more than a very few. More or less isolated and privileged within the ludicrous context, the incongruity can mean anything that makes a person laugh.

This difference accounts for the fact that a poem is susceptible of a limited range of interpretations, while a joke has but one meaning or a million—it really does not make any difference which. A reader, when strongly pressed, may volunteer his own interpretation of a joke, or if he has an open imagination he should be able to concoct others until he grows tired or is stopped. The incongruity in a joke is as private and idiosyncratic as the individual reader himself, while the metaphor in a poem is socially bound, limited in relevance by its relationships to the other parts of the poem. The incongruity may, in fact, be the same in both the joke and the poem, but because we view them from radically different perspectives, they mean quite different things to us. Am I saying, then, that we must think of a joke in some different way, treat it in some different way from the way we are accustomed to treat other kinds of literature? In a word, *yes*. For the materials of a joke are virtually entirely allusive, and since their significance is almost entirely private, that is, unconscious, standard methods of interpretation cannot reveal more than a superficial analysis of jokes. Even if a critic can successfully pierce his own defenses against his own private experience of the joke, that last approach, interesting as it may be, is not germane. The question comes down to this: as a literary critic customarily understands the term, can a joke be interpreted? And the answer is *no*.

I do, of course, read interpretations of jokes with professional interest. Freud, the most important critic of this kind of art, analyzed jokes in a way that no one before had done and no one since can ignore. But as important as his point of view is, his analysis of individual jokes remains a case of special pleading. One may very easily use jokes to put a new edge on a good blade, but there is little question in my mind which is better served, the whetstone or the axe. The problem is not simplified, however, if the critic suspends theorizing in order to provide straight interpretation. If you tell me what you think is funny about a particular joke, I will tell you what I think is funny about it. And if we set ourselves the task of finding variants, there will be no end to our work. And that, according to my understanding of jokes and their ludicrous context, is only as it should be. The function of the joke is to draw up the first idiosyncratic signification that evokes laughter. If that is the case, as I believe it is, and if it is therefore impossible, as I have argued, to arrive at the kind of reliable range of interpretations that we have a right to expect with other kinds of literature, then what can a critic reasonably do with jokes? Offering a single interpretation, of course, is hardly useful and at worst is misleading and pretentious. Discovering all, or even a significant portion of all of the possible idiosyncratic significations is, on the face of it, impossible.

What the critic of jokes can and ought to attempt is the elucidation of a variety of significations, and particularly *opposing* significations. The various interpretations are to be offered not as indicative of a range of reliable meaning, but rather as suggestive of the unique openness of the joke and of its special hospitality towards opposing interpretations. The ludicrous context, characterized as it is by amorality and irrationality, fosters an atmosphere of undiscriminating duality. There is neither right nor wrong, good nor evil—or rather, they are both present, and the joke rewards significations that discover one or the other or both at the same time. This moral and intellectual openness is the secret of the ludicrous context. Any single interpretation of a joke, while it may conform to the critic's personal experience and even conform to acceptable critical methods, still does not recognize the essential open character of that particular joke and of jokes in general. My purpose, then, in analyzing the jokes that follow is to elucidate this principle of openness rather than to provide a representative sample of reliable interpretations as might be attempted successfully with other kinds of literature.

The contents of jokes are generally offered in such a way as not to disguise the ultimate intention.

Two psychiatrists meet at a corner.

This statement can serve almost no other purpose than the introduction of a joke. Virtually automatically we place this statement within a ludicrous context.

Two psychiatrists meet at a corner.

Their names are unnecessary. The cross-streets are not specified. There is no newsstand. No other pedestrians. No distracting details to tie us to circumstantial reality. We automatically accept the meeting of these two professionals without question, for the purpose of the joke, even though there are plenty of questions we might ask. Why were there two of them? Why were they meeting at all? Had they planned to meet, or was it accidental? Why do they meet specifically at a corner and not, say, in the middle of the block, or in a lobby, or in a restaurant? Is the corner especially appropriate to psychiatric meetings, the Oedipal crossroads? Professionally curious, suspicious, even paranoid, do they use the corner for a clear view down all four streets? Or, relativistic and tolerant, perhaps to a fault, do they pick corners as symbolic of their preferring to see all sides at once? Or does the corner simply provide the surprise that catches them unaware?

Two psychiatrists meet at a corner.
One says, "How are you?"

Which "one"? Is there no difference between them? Are they interchangeable? And why does one of them speak at all? Does he know the other one to ask him how he is? If they do know each other, the question asked is merely conventional, the same as saying hello. But if they do not know each other, then this familiar greeting between strangers is incongruously inappropriate:

Two psychiatrists meet at a corner.
One says, "How are you?"
The other replies, "Why do you ask?"

If they are friends, the second psychiatrist perverts the familiar greeting by treating the inquiry literally, apparently taking affront at this prying question: "I am not your patient. How I am is none of your business!" This incongruous enlivening of a cliché is quickened by the public idea of psychiatrists as so obsessed with their method of treatment that a familiar question, dead and buried in a cliché, still inspires an automatically professional reaction. Psychiatrists never like to answer questions themselves. Even, as in this case, when it is not a real, but more like a rhetorical question, the psychiatrist automatically falls into his infuriatingly professional cross-questioning, a man reduced by, victimized by the strength of his skill and training. A simple greeting cannot be offered without provoking an inquisition into motive and causality. The various and even contradictory interpretations derive from the joke's characteristic limitation of distracting details.

In examining the radically open nature of materials in the ludicrous context, it is worth observing that the above joke might be further simplified. The joke, perhaps, need not have indicated *two* psychiatrists, for in reality only the punchline itself must be delivered by a doctor. Yet this change would have been only an apparent simplification, requiring, in fact, more rather than less exposition:

> A man and a psychiatrist meet at a corner.
> The man says, "How are you?"
> The psychiatrist replies, "Why do you ask?"

This more realistic version not only requires more words, it also intrudes a slightly serious realistic consideration by in fact complicating the dramatis personae and by introducing the distracting idea of the man-patient. This joke, then, instead of laughing at psychiatrists, introduces a new victim. In the folklore of patient/psychiatrist relations, it is the patient who is victimized by the doctor's unresponsive questions which the doctor may explain as an essential feature of the treatment. Much more provocatively incongruous is the idea in the original joke that this reticence is not a matter of choice. Psychiatrists cannot communicate even among themselves! Thus, while the joke's specifying two psychiatrists may indicate one more than is strictly necessary to the dramatic situation, we are not concerned here with realistic representation but with the establishment of the best ludicrous context. And for this purpose, two psychiatrists are better than one.

The joke below is No. 118 in the first edition of *Joe Miller's Jests* (London, 1739):

> A melting sermon being preached in a country church, all fell a weeping but one man, who being asked, why he did not weep with the rest? O! said he, I belong to another parish.[1]

This joke belongs to the class of the inadequate response. It isolates the stranger who victimizes himself with his foolish answer. The joke not only isolates him in the singularity of his emotional unresponsiveness—"all fell a weeping but one"—it also confronts him directly and publicly to account for his individual nature. While the situation contains an implicit suspicion of atheism—why did this man alone prove unmoved by the sermon?—the issue of social eccentricity is explicit—why did he alone not join "with the rest"? He is explicitly challenged in his individuality and his separateness. It is perhaps a rudeness thus to confront him and to put him to an awkward and anxious defense of himself. But the joke requires precisely this tension. How, indeed, can one begin to justify one's emotional being— why one laughed here and not there, or why one cried, or why one did not. The question in the joke would be difficult enough were it asked by a friend. But the interlocutor in this joke asks why he did not weep with the rest. The question pits "one" against "all" of "the rest." It is, indeed, the sort of question that may have no acceptable answer.

The answer given is, of course, the punchline of this joke. Before I attempt to analyze this punchline, let me say that in general the punchline is not, as one might presume, the crucial part of the joke.[2] The more important aim of the joke is the establishment of the ludicrous context, without which no situation, no incongruity, no punchline can effect laughter. The Joe Miller joke quoted above can be modernized as follows:

> A beautiful woman passing by a construction site, all the men fell a whistling but one man, who being asked, why he did not whistle with the rest? O! said he, this is my day off.

Other punchlines could work as well: "O! I am the *Times* architecture correspondent," or "O! I'm just writing an article for the *Village Voice*." The fact that a number of punchlines will work as well as or indeed better than the one given does not minimize the importance of the punchline but puts its value in perspective. In terms of relative importance, the development of the situation within the joke is at least as important as the punchline that resolves that situation. If the ludicrous context and the situation are well established, different comedians will be able to supply a variety of effective punchlines.

The punchline under consideration, "I belong to another parish," deserves analysis as one of many possible inadequate reasons for an inappropriate social response. The joke prepares for the foolish an-

swer by means of a loaded, impossible question, of the type, "When
did you stop beating your wife?" The joke poses a question which
is, on the spur of the moment, unanswerable. Why, indeed, is one
different from all the rest? Why, indeed, is one the way one is? Given
an effective ludicrous context, and barring the destruction of this
context by an inept punchline, we would laugh when presented with
any of a number of possible conclusions to this joke. There is an
incongruity in the situation—all weep but one. And there must be
an incongruity in the punchline—here an incongruously inadequate
reason offered in explanation. *Any* inadequate reason that does not
puncture the ludicrous context would allow the context to be fulfilled
by laughter.

In the punchline I am considering, "O! . . . I belong to another
parish," the audience is asked to identify with the speaker who,
embarrassed by being put to an explanation of his behavior, blurts
out a response that by its apparent absurdity and inadequacy victimizes himself and yet by its oblique aptness rewards him. On the face
of it, the reply is as responsive to the question as a non sequitur. This
man, so different from all of the rest, is not, after all an atheist—
nothing so romantic. He is merely a fool. But above this level of self-
ridicule or scorn which may excite or invigorate the laughter of some
members of the audience, there can be felt a more general theme—
a recognition that when we are challenged to explain or justify our
very individuality, whatever we blurt out in our defense must be
foolish, for the source of our one-ness, our difference from the rest,
is beyond the reach of mere explanation and defense. Thus, this
response, while it appears immediately inadequate, may be appreciated positively as a result of the mind's capacity to avoid confrontation by means of an apparently unconscious stratagem. Instead of
confronting the implicit charge of atheism and eccentricity couched
in the interlocutor's question, the man who did not weep evades the
issue by, in effect, ridiculing himself with his foolish answer. He
makes himself a butt. He attacks himself before others can do it first.
It is the strategy of all defensive humor. But while some readers may
enjoy the inventiveness of this strategy simply for its own sake, others
may discover a more wittily positive meaning than the blurted-out
nonsense that it first appears to be. The interlocutor had tried to
isolate him as one against the rest. The butt exploits the attack. He

is not alone—"I belong." He belongs to another parish. He is not an emotional freak, for he does weep when he too joins all the rest of his own fellow parishioners. So he is not alone after all.

The potential in this joke for varieties of meaning depends, as I have argued for all jokes, upon the freedom granted by the ludicrous context. This context is itself susceptible to a great many variations that can effect meaning through, for example, the comedian's choice of gesture and tone of delivery. The non-weeper's response may be slurred by a rural dialect, emphasizing his foolishness; or it may be uttered with an exaggerated diffidence and effeteness of tone, bringing out the yet dormant incongruity between the two kinds of Christians—country and city. In this latter rendition, the punchline would victimize the sophisticated and effete Londoner, but it would also recoil against the bumpkins of the "*country* church" (my italics) who could be made to fall "a weeping" at, of all things, a sermon.

In this connection, it is important to observe the tiny but suggestive incongruity introduced in the metaphoric description of the sermon as a "melting" sermon. This epithet creates a subtle undertow which attacks the mechanical emotionalism of the rural parishioners who may be seen as the hidden butts in this joke. Imagine how the effect would be changed if no adjective were supplied here, and especially if yet another adjective, "country," were also removed, leaving this less suggestive introduction, "A sermon being preached in a church. . . ." While the nonweeper's dry-eyed eccentricity and his ridiculous self-justification would remain intact, we would lose the strong flow of humor back against the automatic weeping of all of the parishioners. We would lose also the stroke of humor against the sermon itself. It was, after all, a "melting" sermon, that is, one written precisely to exploit a particular emotion, which it succeeds in doing with almost universal efficiency. If, in one sense, the non-weeper is put on the spot, in another it is the sermon itself which is exposed as playing upon the all too mechanically exploitable sensibilities of the rural mind. What, we wonder, could this sermon have said that made them all fall to weeping? We can only guess. But it must have been an incredible piece of oratory!

This particular line of inquiry leads to yet another dormant incongruity: the discrepancy between the obvious, theatrically emotional effect and its still secret, veiled cause. I would be curious to hear that sermon, not really to join in the weeping, but to observe how it achieves its extraordinary result. Along this line into the joke, I identify with the alien and dry-eyed witness, just as earlier I stood away from him and laughed at him as the fool. Moreover, the capacity for identification would be greatly affected by the persona who is represented as telling the joke (a minister or a London wit) and to whom (a city or a country audience) it is told. The particular ludicrous context, among the many possible ones for a single joke, depends very heavily for its allusiveness upon what can be called performance values, which can subtly twist the direction of the humor and can even, as I have suggested, create new or enliven dormant incongruities that would not have been apparent in the bare, literal details of the joke.

The catalogue of available meanings for this joke offered here is far from exhaustive. Nor have I made any effort to weigh the value of contradictory meanings. Others which I have not the time and capacity to discover still no doubt lie waiting and available for appreciation beneath the joke's deceptive surface. It is this potential for extensive and utterly idiosyncratic interpretation—what would be called misreading in other genres—that is at the very heart of the nature of jokes. Every analysis of a joke therefore both succeeds and fails, for it is the extraordinary and essential nature of jokes to achieve their effect by means of the easiest irrational mental process available to each member of the audience. If a person were able to retrieve the largely unconscious details of this process, he might interpret the significance of the joke. But his interpretation, while it might succeed in being a perfectly faithful account of his own experience of and relationship to the joke, need not in any respect whatsoever correlate with someone else's equally successful personal interpretation. I have attributed this unique openness to the very genius of jokes, the special character of the ludicrous context which rewards the easiest, fastest, and least rational interpretation with laughter. Given this unique situation, it would be more surprising to find that any two interpretations were alike than to find that they were all different.

Here is another joke which deals with a false or inadequate response:

John-a-Noaks was driving his cart toward Croydon, and growing tired, he fell asleep in it. While he was sleeping someone unhitched his two horses and went away with them. When he awoke and found his horses missing, he exclaimed, "Either I am John-a-Noaks or I am not John-a-Noaks. If I am John-a-Noaks, then I have lost two horses. If I am not John-a-Noaks, than I have found a cart."[3]

This joke may be enjoyed in many lights. We see a man who, confronted with a tremendous loss, suddenly discovers a line of reasoning which describes a gain rather than a catastrophe. But it is a gain that can be entertained only by considering at least the possibility of his annihilation. Within the ludicrous context, the primary incongruity is John-a-Noaks' cavilling response to the theft of his horses. His response is utter nonsense. We already know that "someone unhitched his two horses and went away with them." No pseudological speculation regarding the nature of and the changeability of personal identity can bring back the two horses.

John-a-Noaks is, of course, a fool. After all, he fell asleep in his cart while a thief stole his horses right out of their traces. There is some aberration in his not responding emotionally and mentally to the natural demands of the event he has just experienced. But even more remarkable is the absurdly incongruous nature of the response he does make upon awakening and discovering his loss. Immediately he parodies logical analysis and invents an hypothesis that denies the loss and his own identity. It is incredible that this happy possibility depends upon his seriously entertaining the idea that he may be someone other than himself. And yet he does appear so foolish as actually to believe that he might very possibly be someone else—a very lucky someone who has just found a cart. While from one point of view, this man is a fool, from another he expresses a universal wish for escape from self.

From a psychological point of view this joke can be understood to be about castration. John-a-Noaks is obviously the kind of fool who does not know which end is up anyway. On his trip, probably sexually aroused by the movement of the cart and horses, he easily suffers the loss of his manhood. Indeed, he is left only with the feminine symbol of the cart, which he attempts to rationalize as a gain rather than a loss. So he develops an hypothesis that denies the loss of his manhood, his horses, and positively affirms his new castrated condition as not such a bad thing, in view of the circumstances. Of course, to have gained a cart, i.e., to have become a woman, would mean that he was no longer John-a-Noaks but somebody else—Jane-a-Noaks perhaps?—who has found a cart.

With any other kind of literature, it would be natural to continue our appreciation by analyzing the main character's motivation and the significance of his response. With any other kind of literature, we reasonably expect this endeavor to meet with success. We should be able, for example, to understand what John-a-Noaks meant. Was he simply and literally a fool who meant nothing, who customarily answered reality with nonsense? (Hazlitt records this definition of nonsense: "Sir, it is nonsense to bolt a door with a boiled carrot.")[4] Or did he really mean what he said, that awakening to the consciousness of disaster shocked him into a serious doubt of his own identity? Could it be a dream? Could this really be happening to him? That is, is he really thrust into this state of personal uncertainty, or, quite aware of himself, is he consciously and intentionally making his own joke about his loss? Yes to all of these questions—and no to all of them, and forget the contradictions.

Contradictions are inevitable and necessary in jokes. Other kinds of literature would likely be harmed by a context that permitted such a wide range of significances and even contradictions. Not so with jokes. We do not need to be able to know whether John-a-Noaks is a fool or a philosopher. The more potential significances that his remark can inspire the better. The central incongruity is like a vortex, powerfully drawing to itself not only appropriate significances and emotions (as in a poetic metaphor), but all the intellectual and emotional associations it can—conscious or unconscious, cumulative or self-contradictory. It makes no difference, for they all are welcome. So the joke about John-a-Noaks carries a special and a personal pleasure and meaning to all who laugh at it—including literary critics and teamsters, philosophers and Freudian psychologists.

In contrast to other kinds of literature, jokes cannot be full of realistically organized details. There must be ample psychical room, a wide openness to idiosyncratic, personal signification. There must be room for the audience's imagination to intensify the characters and the incongruity with private significance. We can study this feature in the following joke: "In Edinburgh two burglars smashed a jeweler's window. They were arrested when they came back for the brick."[5]

There is room in this joke for a reader's mind to enlarge upon the obvious points of Scottish frugality and a criminal's capacity for stupidity. When I first "got" this joke, my mind immediately filled up the blanks, intensifying the characters and the incongruity. I particularly enjoy now the provocative detail that there were *two* burglars. This fact increases the nationalistic slur (*all* Scotsmen are cheapskates), but more importantly for me, it opens an imagined dialogue between the two thieves who, in the heat of their escape, suddenly realize their carelessness in leaving the brick, and immediately, and sagely, as with one mind, agree to return to the scene of their crime.

It is also possible to enjoy the strategy of the Edinburgh police who, knowing the temperament of their fellow countrymen, as a matter of course and standard operating procedure, staked out the brick. I also like to imagine that the two thieves take their arrest with resignation—you win some, you lose some—the outcome of the gamesmanship played between clever detectives and master criminals. Here are wise fools, thieves who smash windows yet have respect for their tools, a left brick. It is as important to them as the jewels themselves. Wise men, fools, devoted to details or lost in them, neat in their work regardless of the consequences or victims of their national character—whatever interpretation we may apply to them, these are not men so much as idealizations, hyperbolic images of irrelevancy. Like all characters in jokes, they are not just stereotypes, but two-dimensional figures cut out of mirror glass. The general outlines are given; the surface, however, shows not them but us, and reflects us darkly, a kaleidoscope of obscure, pleasurable secretly personal imagery.

The ludicrous context permits this wide personal signification, as in this joke which begins, "A beautiful brunette has a red-headed baby."[6] The beginning of the joke keeps its contents within the range of ludicrousness, unless, perhaps, we are obsessively and fanatically serious geneticists. The style, or rhetoric with which this joke begins tends to preserve the subject matter within a ludicrous frame of mind, and tends to prevent its acceptance in any of the many nonhumorous ways in which it is capable of being understood. The stylistic device which introduces this joke is generalized exemplification. The material is presented as if it were an example of some point being discussed. This is a rhetorical device remarkably common in joke telling:

A travelling salesman stops at a lonely farmhouse . . .
A fashionable lady was crossing the street . . .
This cop and this hooker . . .

The material of the joke is introduced on a stage kept bare of all but essential elements. The scene is purified, abstracted from the fullness of detail and from the logical complexities that might indicate that a serious appeal to our mind and feelings were being made. "A beautiful brunette" is called into view. Why? and why not a blonde? Or an ugly brunette? The style sounds like that of a school puzzle: "A man walks 3 miles per hour on a level surface, but only 1.4 miles per hour uphill; how far . . . ?" Now the student may refuse to accept the context: "A" man? Is that a tall or a fat man? And how steep is the hill? Pity his teacher. Every statement is, to some degree, susceptible of misinterpretation; but no statement is immune to willful misreading. There can be no possibility of communication when a reader cannot or will not adjust his understanding of the content to the context in which it is offered. If the reader insists upon asking the name of the beautiful brunette, he has ceased to regard this matter within a ludicrous context. Thus, that pointed word which introduces millions of jokes, the article, "A," helps to support the ludicrous context in its aspect of irrelevancy. As in the school puzzle, the character introduced is to be understood only within the very special context of joke or puzzle. The details offered—the facts that she is beautiful and brown-haired, and that he walks at 3 miles per hour— are not to be understood to have any wider relevancy than the extremely specialized and artificial demands made by the rest of the joke or puzzle. The details of the joke stand, protected by the ludicrous context, in a specially privileged position, directing their relevance towards the special needs of the joke itself.

The context of art and the context of reality are quite different, though it is possible for naive readers and many critics to mistake them. Joe Miller records a joke about the sort of rube who might confuse the two spheres of activity:

Two countrymen, who had never seen a play in their lives, nor had any notion of it, went to the Theatre in Drury-Lane, when they placed themselves snug in the corner of the middle-gallery; the first music played, which they liked well enough; then the second, and the third to their great satisfaction. At length the curtain drew up, and three or four actors entered to begin the play, upon which one of them cried to the other, "Come, Hodge, let's be going, ma'haps the gentlemen are talking about business."[7]

In the joke's terms, only a fool would mistake pleasure for business. While art may portray business, no one really wins or loses in the conduct of it. The mental context or state of mind that experiences a work of art is and must be quite different from the state of mind that experiences reality. Art engages a general state of mind called imagination, with which the audience in part shares the writer's aim, to recreate his version of reality. But this imaginative version, no matter how faithfully recreated, can never completely achieve reality, since it is radically different in kind from it. The pleasure, and indeed the pain of the imagination, are singularly different from the pleasures and pains of reality. And to that extent, the matter of art has a kind of relevance that is directed more to the nature of the imaginative experience, while the matter of reality has an imminent, practical, and decisive relevance.

This is not to say that the mental context of our imaginative experience of art is far removed from the mental context of our practical experience of reality, or that the kinds of mental processes which occur in these contexts are generally different. Certainly these areas of differing kinds of experience share some common boundaries or else are served by corridors of communication. Art and the imaginative experience it effects can have a share of influence on the realistic sphere. Indeed, some forms of art more than others, satire, for example, claim this kind of influence as their main purpose. Without entering into a discussion of the validity of this claim, it is obvious and pertinent to note that jokes, far from making any similar claim, make no claim whatsoever other than the excitement to the pleasure of laughter. The matter of a joke makes the least possible claim to relevance to the experience of reality. Not only does a joke share in the specially privileged situation of art by aiming at the broad state of mind called imagination, to which all forms of art appeal, but the matter of a joke also aims at a particular site within the imagination I call the locus of the ludicrous context, which of all aesthetic contexts is least connected to the realistic and relevant concerns of rationality, morality, and work.

When a comedian tells us that "A beautiful brunette has a red-headed baby," we do not expect that it will have any direct, realistic relevance. Nor do we accept the announcement as having the slightest iota of practical informational value. Even were the statement simplified into "A woman has a baby," we still are left with the bald formulaic beginning for a multitude of jokes. We are still timelessly in the everlasting present, confronted with generic woman. The detail, "brunette," adds a fact whose only significance is to function as one pole of an incongruity completed by the word "red-headed." The apposition of "black-haired" and "blonde" would almost equally well serve the purposes of the joke—almost as well, because red-headedness adds an extra tincture of sexuality. Similarly, the word "beautiful" serves not to particularize her biographically, but to further stereotype her sexual attractiveness. There is no necessity to accord this woman and her child any more biographical or realistic detail than is strictly required to effect an incongruity in a ludicrous context—the essential requirements for laughter. The present tense further establishes the already generalized details of the joke in an idealized moment forever frozen in their incongruousness.

Any reader who is faster on the uptake than refrigerated honey already knew several pages ago when I first mentioned the introduction to the joke that it concerned sexual promiscuity. But since countless jokes begin with this same rhetorical technique of generalized exemplification, it is worth observing that this introduction might just as probably come from a lecture on genetics as from a joke: "A brunette has a red-headed baby. Genetically speaking . . ." I will not belabor the point about the crucial importance of the ludicrous context to jokes, nor will I further prolong the reader's curiosity to hear the punchline whose point he has already, though not entirely accurately anticipated.

> A beautiful brunette has a red-headed baby. "Ah," says the doctor, "father red-headed?" "I don't know," says the brunette. "He didn't take off his hat."[8]

The beginning, or exposition of the joke introduces a mild incongruity and supports the ludicrous context for which cues had been previously supplied. Within the ludicrous context, this mild incongruity is itself funny. While it would not normally cause outright laughter, it would create or broaden the smile which signifies the forepleasure of laughter, the anticipation with which we respond to the successful establishment of a ludicrous context.

We are prepared, then, for a joke about the brunette's sexual relations. The doctor, hardly a flesh-and-blood character himself, is introduced only to raise the question that is on all of our minds, and at the same time to satisfy at least a partial wish to embarrass the beautiful brunette by creating an awkward confrontation concerning the woman's moral character and her child's legitimacy. It is an apparently harmless question, but fraught with potentially malicious implication. The way the woman begins her answer at first seems to confirm our intuition about how this joke would go. "I don't know." The slut, she does not know which of her lovers actually fathered this child, or else, she has such a partiality for red-haired lovers that she could not say who, among them, was responsible. Yet after the well-placed pause, the joke turns abruptly away from the moral theme of promiscuity towards which it had been apparently proceeding. The woman is oblivious to the implicit menace of the doctor's question. For her, it was not a question of adultery, or of the number of lovers, or of a perverse fetish for red-haired men. The joke finally turns on the anonymity, the impersonality, the speed, and the strategy of that form of sexual encounter known as "the quickie."

It seems to me that the main incongruity of this joke concerns the implicit moral threat of the exposition as reinforced by the doctor's apparently innocent question and the total and surprising lack of moral content and tone in her answer. Incongruously, she ignores or does not see any threat and she merely responds to the question in totally amoral, practical terms, as simply a request for information. The father is not among her acquaintances. Her relationship with him had been at once intimate and remarkably perfunctory. She is exceedingly naive to miss the moral menace of the doctor's question—in which case her answer belongs to the class of punchlines mentioned earlier, the inadequate response. Or she is extremely self-assured, sees the moral threat, and refuses to treat her sexual life on a moral plane. She is extraordinarily advanced in her sexual shamelessness or she is literally a dunce, "I don't know." The precise answer to this critical problem cannot be known and, moreover, does not matter so long as the reader apprehends her character in such a way that he comes to the pleasure of laughter. It is, I repeat, not possible to define precisely what her attitude is towards this strange lover who did not (would not? could not?) take off his hat. Was she surprised? Amused? Angry? Did she not care one way or the other? All men are a little peculiar. He wore a hat. So what? It could have been a baseball uniform. And if she were a Freudian, she might have found the phallic image of the hat a perfectly appropriate symbol for a man to wear in the dreamscape of a sexual joke. Whatever her attitude, the reader is left with a remarkably incongruous image of a naked (partly clothed? unzipped?) man busy in the act of love while wearing a hat (boater? porkpie? ten gallon? yarmulke? derby?). My point here, as before, is that the joke situates within a ludicrous context relatively broadly defined incongruities so that different readers may contribute their own extremely personal significations for the sake of laughter.

As I have argued earlier, it is impossible to analyze the precise and hidden avenues of thought and emotion that for a particular joke effect laughter in a member of an audience. It is the very nature of the ludicrous context (which the various elements of the joke itself confirm and support) to allow the widest possible range of personal association and idiosyncratic, unconscious interpretation of the incongruous materials within the joke. The potential for human drama in the joke under consideration is enormous. The situation and characters given are certainly capable of amplification and expansion into other genres—the short story, novel, play, etc. Within these genres we would have infinitely less trouble and a reasonable chance of success in arriving at fairly reliable interpretations. But it is the very nature of the ludicrous context and the joke's economy of detail, its suggestive and inviting openness to safe, free, and personal significance that allows us this particular form of enjoyment and prevents the same kind and degree of interpretation we use in the other kinds of art. In jokes, what a critic must aim for is not a single interpretation, nor even possible competing or opposite interpretations, but an extremely wide range, indeed, whole galaxies of such dichotomous points of view. Perhaps it is possible for me, after thorough analysis, to discover with some reliability the reason why I laugh at a particular joke. But I would not be able to do the same for you. You have your own reasons. The acceptance of the ludicrous context is responsible for this essential effect. It is as if the comedian and the audience have struck an implicit bargain: I will tell you something funny and you will laugh, and none of us shall be the wiser.

Of all the forms of art that serve laughter, jokes are the most numerous, the purest, and perhaps the most ancient species. To say this is to show no disrespect to those authors who have employed the ludicrous context in parts of or indeed as the medium for entire works of art, even the least of which can lay claim to a degree of longevity that mocks the impermanence of individual jokes. Much of what we know about how the ludicrous context affects jokes can also be profitably applied to our analysis of larger works of art in which the ludicrous context operates during the range, say, of a single joke, or indeed extends throughout the entire work. It is to this task that I now turn—a task more traditional and directly challenging to the theoretical and practical implications of the idea of the ludicrous context.

CHAPTER FOUR

Lenny Bruce and Extreme Comedy

THE LUDICROUS context functions best in jokes when it is simply taken for granted. But a work of extended comedy may be said ultimately to be about the exploration and articulation of the ludicrous context itself—about the way the ludicrous context is created to confine the subject matter within the bounds of humor. More or less, the context in individual jokes plays a relatively passive role, but in extended works of comedy it becomes as active a force as, say, the main character or even the perceived author.

A successful individual joke by definition establishes a functional ludicrous context. But it is a ludicrous context that lacks, because it does not need, any distinctive, individual tone or quality. Such a blunt cue as, "Here's a funny joke I heard yesterday," may be enough to establish the ludicrous context, but single jokes generally do not contain enough cues to convey a unique contextual tone. This limitation, of course, is absent in extended works of comedy. A comedian's nightclub performance of a considerable number of jokes can develop a context that is distinctly original. Very successful tellers of jokes certainly have a recognizable contextual style that does not necessarily depend upon the dramatis personae, the content, or the kind of plotting employed in their jokes.

Let me attempt now to expand my analysis of individual jokes to deal with the extended work of a single comedian. In addition to illustrating the nature of a particular contextual style, Lenny Bruce also presents a special opportunity for exploring the differences between satire and comedy. Bruce is, of course, an extreme case—a comedian who carried comedy almost beyond the borders of the genre. It is the very extreme nature of this case that makes it especially instructive.

An appropriate place to begin is the long sustained monologue on Frank Dell, perhaps Bruce's most fully developed fictional character, and Dell's disastrous performance at the Palladium Theatre. Bruce begins in his own voice, disclaiming the myth of playing to a class audience. He then becomes Frank Dell, "Dean of Satire and Mimicry," who believes that his whole life would be meaningless if he did not play a "class room."[1] His agent tries to argue or humor him out of this obsession, but Frank is a driven man: "Look, I'm tired of playing the toilets, man. I've had it." Of course it is a mistake. Frank is fine in the lounges of Las Vegas for decent money—"Is that spit?" his agent argues. This agent, an insufficient creature in almost every way, does comprehend the hard realities of the business. His expertise is in the dispassionate calculation of the probabilities of supply and demand. His view of the world is brutally limited, but he is absolutely right about Frank Dell. We are not encouraged to like the agent—Lenny Bruce gives him the busy Broadway agent's voice that is capable of sudden modulations from roughness into transparent motherly love: "Sweetie baby bubby, sweetie." We do not like him, but he is right and Frank Dell is wrong.

The music conductor at the Palladium also knows immediately at the rehearsal that Dell will fail. When he sees Frank's list of the standard show biz impressions, he mumbles, "Same crap week after week . . . disgusting." Frank apparently asks what he said, but the conductor replies acidly, "I'm sure you do the impressions different— you probably do them as children." The conductor, the agent, and later the house booker at the Palladium, Val Parnell, all see Frank's limitations. They are the bottom line—reality. They know exactly what will happen, and they are right. Frank Dell's performance, therefore, stacks up as a confrontation between his tremendous need for recognition and acceptance and the reality against which all wishes must struggle.

The comic energy of this piece derives from the fact that Dell has pushed himself into a situation where he cannot succeed. His schlock American jokes just will not go over for a British vaudeville audience. His impressions—"Show Business Heaven"—his pseudohip shtick— "Hep Smoke a Reefer"—his tired Las Vegas jokes—"walk right into the propeller"—none of it will work. But it is not his inadequacy alone that kills him. Fate has conspired the show bill so that Frank

follows the singer, Georgia Gibbs, who is absolutely smashing. She
has the audience in the palm of her hand. Song after song. Then she
goes into her "Tribute-to-Sophie-Tucker-Hello-God number." And
finally, for her encore, she pitches her voice deep towards lachrymose
sentimentality as she gravely invokes "a moment of silence—for the
poor boys who went to Dunkirk—and never came back." Lenny
Bruce cackles in amazement at the incredible fatalism of Frank's bad
luck: "You couldn't follow that except with a leper on the Art Baker
Show!" But Frank has to go on. This is his last chance, the one he
begged and sobbed for. His programmed "bits," his mechanical patter—"I got it down, man—24 minutes of dynamite"—they didn't
work before, and now, "Ring-a-ding, into the toilet for good this
time. Forget it. Not one laugh."

The stony silence has made Frank desperate. He keeps trying, bit
after bit, but "It's granite out there: Jefferson, Washington, Lincoln—
forget it! It's, like, not there, but keep punching and punching
away. . . ." Desperate with self-pity and rage, Frank suddenly tries
to play upon the audience's conscience: "It's a nice way to treat an
American, folks, thanks a lot for that. I was in the service too guys,
if that means anything to you." He's drowning. "Nothing. They're
looking at him. Mean faces. They're staring up there—fifteen
hundred people—an oil painting." This scenario is not immediately
comic. A mediocre comedian out of false pride has thrust himself into
a situation in which he must fail. This is a plot that can go either
way—towards comedy or tragedy.

The closeness of the balance makes Bruce's final version share the
flavor of both, but the factor which keeps it within the borders of the
ludicrous context is Bruce's artistic exaggeration, which helps to establish the context for comedy. Most notable is the language of hyperbole—Georgia Gibbs' catch-all "Tribute," and the "oil painting."
Bruce, as narrator, can be heard taking audible delight, chuckling
over his own strokes of wit. And the audience responds to the cues,
laughing no doubt at the surprising, incongruous purity of the imagery. Here are pictures not to be found in reality, yet partaking of
it by means of purification and exaggeration. So these are images
which we can understand because they have a share in reality, but
we can also laugh at them because more importantly they have a
larger share in fantasy, fiction, and exaggeration, a circumstance

which renders them harmless in a way. Thus the audience responds
not to Frank Dell's catastrophic evening at the Palladium, but to the
author of this disaster, Lenny Bruce, who, unlike Dell, is obviously
in control, creating and exaggerating this event.

We understand this process in our own lives: when a day goes
badly for us, we are fretful, but when it is perfectly awful, we may
surrender to the humor of the situation, laughing at the artful con-
catenation of events which conspire to create a vision of gloom so
untainted by optimism, so ideally bad, that we are perversely and
aesthetically delighted with the artfulness of the exaggeration. In
short, when events become so hyperbolically painful, we may dis-
sociate ourselves from the content and rather enjoy the style which
so perfectly orders the content towards an idealized awfulness. We
resituate these same events in a new context, a ludicrous context.
The result is that we are led away from the sad contents of reality
towards a sympathetic appreciation of the style which contains them.
There occurs a progression from real to ideal, from fact to fiction,
from content to context. This progress releases reality's painful grasp
upon our hearts and frees us to humorously appreciate the artful
arrangement rather than the content of painful material.

In Lenny Bruce's Palladium Concert piece, we appreciate his verbal
artistry and wit, symbolizing his control over and superiority to Frank
Dell's disastrous performance. But just as attractive as the verbal
control and sharing in its exaggeration towards hyperbole is Bruce's
control over and exaggeration of the entire scenario. It begins with
Dell's impatience over his lagging career, the comfortable but narrow
rut he is in, and his willingness to gamble it all away for a chance at
the respectability of a "class room." It cannot happen. From the
beginning, Lenny Bruce leaves Dell to slide down the way to destruction. It is not a graceful exit. All the way down, Dell is "punching,
punching," digging his nails in, white. Failure is inevitable, but Dell
pounds the sullen audience, bit after bit, with his stale and, to them,
incomprehensible shtick. He even insults them. Then, desperately,
he plays on their pity. Finally, driven nearly berserk with rage and
frustration, his mind fastens on an incredible stratagem: "All right
folks, there's another little bit here. Screw Ireland folks, how about
that?" Immediately from up in the balcony, a voice through cupped
hands booms back: "That's the funniest thing you've said all night,

boy. That's right! Screw Ireland! Screw Ireland! . . . Screw the Irish. They Stole the Grail!" The irrational stratagem on the stage triggers the insane race and religious prejudice slumbering in the audience. The ensuing riot completely destroys the interior of the theater, while the sounds of rage and destruction pursue Dell into his dressing room where he stoops over the toilet bowl. Bruce mimics the sounds of vomiting. It is over.

The catastrophic denouement again borders between tragedy and comedy. In the tragic formula, we see a man driven by false pride into a situation which fatalistically impels him towards disaster. There is no exit. And, comically, we laugh at the deliberate, hyperbolic perversity of fate: not only are the dice loaded against him, but the circle is made of shills, and the money is counterfeit. There is no hope against these odds. Really, there are no odds at all, no possibility. His fate is signed and sealed. But Frank Dell does not know this—only God, Lenny Bruce, and us. So Frank keeps trying, "punching, punching." He has unravelled the whole ball of string which curls around his feet. Now he is left holding the end. The audience has become his enemy, the inflexible material upon which he must hack out his dream. But it is a material intractable to the artist's wishes. He grows angry, insults the audience, pleads with them. Desperate with frustration, his career unreeling before his eyes, he must get a reaction from them. His stratagem, arising spontaneously like a free association, is to provoke their anger. The response is more than he could expect or wish—a rolling tide of hatred that destroys the theater and his career.

Bruce's humor here turns on the motif of the failed stratagem. Spontaneous and inspired tactics are natural material for comedy, exploding the tension of the apparently insoluble problem. A stratagem, as used here, is what ordinary man resorts to in the face of overwhelming odds. Strategy, on the other hand, is an abiding workaday guardian of the wise man, a cure against problems that can be foreseen and with prudence solved. So while we may nod approval at strategy, we laugh with delight at the stratagem. But Frank Dell's stratagem had an effect exactly opposite from his intention. In a stroke of brilliant self-annihilation, he has turned a bad situation into a holocaust, snatched disaster from the jaws of simple defeat.

Thus the final stroke of Bruce's humor is about the perversity of the human mind. Frank Dell had been following his instincts from the very beginning. He was wrong then. His whole performance was wrong. And his last joke was irretrievably wrong. He could not have done worse if he had engaged a team of assassins to blow up the theater while he was on stage. The humor here coincides with the general humor on cosmically bad luck. Sometimes events conspire to make everything turn out so badly that we must laugh at the hyperbolic artistry of fate. And sometimes our every effort to save the disaster works only to increase its size and impact. You replace the fallen can in the supermarket and the next thing you know, the manager and the stockboys are digging you out of the avalanche of the weekly special. Frank Dell had that kind of a day. The humor is cosmic—it tells how we are made ridiculous by a complex succession of events, accidents really, and how what should be of most aid to us in such straits, our mental powers, most betray us.

Bruce's humor is about the impulsiveness of the imagination. Especially as an artist, he understood that when the imagination is placed under some tension it is capable of the most surprisingly creative outbursts. Bruce, who ad libbed much of his material before an audience, obviously knew this kind of sudden creativity. It is capable of producing the *bon mot*, the apt characterization, the flash of insight. But by the same token, judging from the Frank Dell portrait, Bruce must have also known the bad night and the dull audience; certainly there were the drunken audiences in cheap nightclubs who waited only for the strippers. To gain their attention, in desperation, Bruce sometimes undressed and went naked on stage. Surely if under pressure the imagination is capable of achieving images of perfection, it may also achieve the opposite: that is to say, not just dull ordinary mediocrity, but images that are perfectly inapt, perfectly awful. If the mind can run impulsively towards greatness, it can also plunge into the opposite, a kind of negative creativity, a theatrical nihilism. Frank Dell's desperation produced a flash of this kind of perverse genius. A mediocre comedian, but under pressure to win approval, he had invented a stratagem that failed on an enormous scale. He had abandoned his canned patter and had plunged into his imagination. It was probably the first, and considering the response, the last truly inventive act of his career. To be sure, the imagination contains the energy of life, but its effects cannot always be predicted. Dell wanted the audience to go crazy for him. And they did, with a vengeance.

The stratagem is a device that appears throughout Bruce's work. It forms the punchline for his extended fantasy about a prison rebellion called "Father Flotsky's Triumph." The scene opens with the Warden's voice through a bull horn: "Give up Dutch and we'll meet any reasonable demands you men want—except the vibrators." Can you imagine how those demands would have been drawn up in the movies of the thirties and forties? They would have gotten the editor of the prison newspaper, Charles Bickford, probably, to write them out, because nobody would have known how to spell "vibrators." And Edward G. Robinson, probably would have been nagging, "Don't forget them vibrators!" In Lenny Bruce's version, the warden thinks that he might put down the insurrection "if we kill a few for an example." But his staff is extremely inefficient, and he has to prod them away from their card game. Then they cannot find the ammunition. "The bullets?" the warden replies, "Look in back of my brown slacks. . . ."

It is a silly scene, including the amiable Father Flotsky himself, with the Barry Fitzgerald voice, and the quaint homilies: "There's an old story, that once a boy goes the bad road, the good road is hard to follow, when the good road is hard to follow, the bad road opens when the good road closes." But when his counsel fails—after all, he has got an investment in this scene too—he turns vicious: "They're all no good the lot of them. Pour it in. Kill them all!" It looks like another Attica until a voice suddenly croons out. It is Kiki the hospital attendant. Bruce does the voice of exaggerated homosexuality—with nasality, lisp, lilt, and all: "Dutch, lithen to me bubby!" Kiki reminds Dutch of all the bed baths and rubdowns he gave and he tells the rioters to cool it. His advice is taken, and the scene ends with his reading off his own demands to a tired and beaten warden. First, "A gay bar in the west wing." And the capper, "I wanna be the Avon representative in the prison!" Both punchlines—about vibrators and the gay bar—humorously undercut the pretensions of the Hollywood genre of prison films. But even more, they display a basically human response to the inhuman pressures of reality. For Lenny Bruce, as in the Palladium Concert piece, when a need is frustrated, it asserts itself explosively, apparently irrationally, like a non sequitur. The stratagem is one version of this impulsiveness.

It asserts itself again and economically as part of a piece called "White Collar Drunks." A respectable looking man—completely

smashed but not wanting to show it—tries to con a free drink. He
sits down at the bar and immediately complains to the bartender:
"Don't you think it's time that the house bought a drink?" A little
while later he accuses the bartender of taking away the drink he never
bought. These are transparent, pathetic ploys, almost not worth the
name of stratagem, but they show how much he wants a drink. The
scene is interrupted by another chiseler, a real heavy drunk, his voice
gravelly, aggressive, ready to belch. This is his incredible, blunt con:
"I'm with the FBI. I may have to take you in if you don't give me 29
cents for some wine. You wanna go downtown, or you wanna gimme
the money?" Can he believe that such an outlandish stratagem will
actually work? It almost doesn't matter. When the mind does not get
what it needs, it grinds into itself, pushing for some angle, some
shortcut to satisfaction.

In a similar vein, Bruce sets a middle-class white citizen next to a
black man at a suburban cocktail party. He tries to strike up a friendly
conversation, but his mind, driven by prejudice and a perverse fatalism, invariably fastens on exactly the wrong thing to say: "That
Joe Louis was a helluva fighter." He also wants to do the right thing
and invite the man over to dinner: "I wanna have you over the house
but I got a bit of a problem . . . I got a sister . . . and I hear that you
guys . . . I hear you got some perfume you put on 'em and they make
you do it to 'em . . . Is that true, there's no perfume you put on 'em?
They just do it to you?" Like Frank Dell, the more he talks, the more
he wants to be liked, the worse matters get. When a stratagem fails,
it does not fail by halves. It is perfectly awful, dismal. And when it
succeeds, there is nothing more fortuitous and luminous. The real
trouble is, there is no predictable relationship between intention and
accomplishment, between what one wants and what one in fact gets.

It is true that the result often mocks the intention, and this is one
of the sources of Bruce's comedy, but it must be emphasized that the
result never utterly stifles the wish. Though the wish often meets
with rebuffs from the world, and even from the mind itself as it tries
in vain for satisfaction, the wish survives as the driving force of the
personality, the source of all hope and all energy. Lenny Bruce said
it quite simply: it was all "Look at me, Ma!" It was all for love, for
acceptance. Lenny Bruce tried to explain this wish in sexual terms
in a long didactic piece about marriage. He was trying to explain to

women why men have different sexual needs, and why women should not blame them for merely physical infidelities. "Guys" are different, he says, because they "detach." "Like a lady can't go through a plate glass window and go to bed with you five seconds later. But guys can have head-on collisions with Greyhound busses. In disaster areas—everybody's laying dead on the highway, and on the way to the hospital in the ambulance, the guy makes a play for the nurse." Now Bruce imitates the voice of outraged womankind:

Woman: How could he do a thing at a time like that?
Man: (*mumbling, embarrassed*) Well, I got horny.
Woman: (*outraged*) What?!
Man: I got hot.
Woman: How can you be hot when your foot was cut off and you're
    . . . dead?
Man: I don't know.
Woman: He's an animal! He got hot with his foot cut off!
Man: (*broken, ashamed*) I guess I'm an animal. . . .
Woman: What did you get hot at?
Man: The nurse's uniform. . . .

Bruce zips into another sexual fantasy about men trapped on a desert island: "You put guys on a desert island, they'll do it to mud." Then he imagines the guy's wife showing up and catching him doing it to mud, and berating him for being a pervert, and telling him to get his mud to make his dinner for him. Bruce explains to the women: "You can't get angry at them. You can't wanna leave them for that." There is no guaranteed right time, right place, or right way to want anything in this world. When wishes make their journey into the world, reality treats them as if they were irrelevant. How do you live in such a world?

One way is the con. If there is no impeccable system of reward and punishment, then you are left to figure out some plan for each situation. Ad hoc. So you try to measure the direction and force of your wishes and the resistance of the world to them, and hope to find a loophole through the difficulties. Philosophers may square the circle. What is needed in reality is an angle on the corner—a percentage against the uncertainty of fity-fifty. That's the con—a carefully conceived and elegantly executed incision through the corner. But if the shortcut opens suddenly, fortuitously, and if on impulse alone we plunge into the opening, that is the stratagem. Bruce's imagination abounded with examples. His biographer, Albert Goldman, has called the con one of the basic metaphors of Bruce's mind, reducing every-thing—religion, the law courts, love—to the narrow perspective of the shingleman or the Broadway agent.[2] But what ought to be said also is that this association and this reduction are in no way pejorative or demeaning. Bruce does not hold up the dice for us to see the shaved corner and complain, "Look what cheats there are among us!" No, the shaving shows what kind of pain it is living in a fifty-fifty world, and how we need an angle to improve the odds. It is as much a testimony of human presence as the great pyramids. Lenny Bruce, once a shingleman himself and a solicitor for bogus charities, understood the con from the inside out.

Perhaps Bruce's best dramatization of the con, and certainly his most controversial, was his piece called "Religions Inc." Its premise is the summit meeting called by the religious leaders of the nation and attended by the day workers in the field. The metaphor is the corporate convention, and religion is seen as Big Business, a con for packing the suckers into a tight circle around the snake oil wagon and fleecing them for all they're worth. But this is no penny ante con. The spokesman, A.A., comes prepared with charts and statistics: "The graph here tells the story. . . . For the first time in twelve years, Catholicism is up 9 points. Judaism is up 15. The Big P, the Pente-costal, is startin' to move finally." Later in the meeting, and getting deeper into business, a question arises about what to do with a val-uable tract of "the Heavenly Land" that has just been acquired—Chavez Ravine. Since it is a matter of real estate, Rabbi Weiss is called on for his expert opinion. "I think we should subdivide," he says. On a smaller scale, A.A. announces the new line for the coming year from the religious novelty house: "the gen-yew-ine Jewish-star-lucky-cross an' cigarette-lighter combined; an' we got the kiss-me-in-the-dark mehzoozoo . . . an' these wonderful lil' cocktail napkins with some helluva sayings there—'Another martini for Mother Cabrini.'" Things like that.

It's all a big con, and A.A., knowing he is addressing an audience of six thousand accomplished con men, prudently issues a warning: "You know, the commissioner promised there'd be no individual hustlin', you know. I mean, let's make the scene together, because,

like, if we burn ourselves, where're we gonna end up, you dig?"
However, because he is among colleagues, he can lower his guard
enough to reminisce sanguinely about how far he has come: "I just
was talkin' to Billy this afternoon. I said, 'Billy, you come a long way,
sweetie, long way.' Who woulda thought back in '31–we were hustlin' baby pictures then, an' shingles and sidin'. . . . An just like *that*
we come on, you know? The Gideon, *Bop!*, and there we were."
Lenny Bruce continues the metaphor of the con as he introduces the
best character in the piece, "a great man and a great holy roller,
Oral!"

Oral has an incredibly flexible voice that drawls into moody con-
spiratorial whispers or booms with power and confidence—a pas-
sionate voice, totally unselfconscious. Yet he knows that some people
do not like him, maybe for his preaching style, his "ranting and
raving," or for his coarseness, or for his eccentricities, like his holy
rolling greeting to A.A., "Here, boy, have a snake!" He knows some
people think he's dumb, but it doesn't bother him: "Maybe I'm dumb.
That's it. That old dumbbell up there. Ha Ha Ha. There's the dummy.
Why don't you all have a laugh. That's right. Laugh at him. Ho Ho
Ho Ho. There's the dummy. I'm dumb. Ha Ha Ha Ha! Yes I'm dumb.
I got two Lincoln Continentals! That's how goddam dumb I am! I'm
dumber 'n Hell. I don't know how much a whole lot of nines are."
Here it is, the pride in achievement, in the successful con. The scene
closes with a phone call from the newly elected Pope. Oral picks up
the phone and bellows out his greetings in the jive, hipster, show-
biz argot: "Hello Johnny! What's shakin' baby?" The rest of the dialogue continues in this show-biz lingo, as Oral gives the Pope the
good news that he got him an eight-page layout for Viceroy: "The
new Pope is a thinking man." Oral thought, correctly, that the Pope
wouldn't go for the tattoo to get Marlboro. But the Pope does seem
interested in Oral's tour package capped by an appearance on the Ed
Sullivan show. Their negotiations, however, are interrupted by a
request from Billy. Oral asks the Pope, "Billy wants to know whether
you can get him a deal on one of them Dago sportscars." Of course,
what we are impressed with immediately is the audacity of the humor
characterizing the Pope and the other thinly disguised religious leaders as show-biz personalities or only barely ethical businessmen.
Everything is reduced, as it were, to the comedian's own level. But

we have yet to answer why this reduction is not derogatory or satiric of religion.

Our own response to Lenny Bruce's work provides the best evidence for answering this problem. We laugh. But surely not at the idea that organized religion might be regarded as being run very much like a big business. The idea is so trite as to be capable of producing a kind of nervous laughter in only the most sheltered minds. Moreover, there is no real humor in the idea that sacred institutions may be overrun by scoundrels. In short, religion only provides the occasion or the background for the joke. What, in fact, provokes our humor is the incredible, hyperbolic audacity of the characters Bruce portrays. For example, the sacred idea of "the Heavenly Land"—whatever conventional or even private associations that idea is capable of raising in our minds, one of them is certainly not the concept of a land grab scheme in the Chavez Ravine and subdivision of the lots for tract housing. The humor develops out of the background tension arising from the desperate uncertainties about life and the nature of death for which religion attempts to provide answers. And the acceptance of these answers is the outcome of spiritual growth and the triumph of faith. But the sudden and delightful humor is that Lenny Bruce's characters have found a shorter way. Subdivide! Would it were that simple. But that is exactly the pleasure we have in Bruce's characters. For them it is that simple. And for a time, we cheerfully identify with them and share in their incredibly direct shortcut to paradise.

If the Pope Himself is concerned only about public relations, his 8 × 10 glossies, and whether his Jewish nose gives him away—and who is in a better position to know what *really* matters?—then we certainly have nothing serious spiritually to fear from life or death. Everything is simple and on the surface. And if, like Oral, most of us are given to pause before stating how much a lot of nines are, we can all count two Lincoln Continentals in the driveway. The reduction to materialism satisfies a wish that we all to some degree share. In Lenny Bruce's imaginary world, we gratefully leave St. Augustine to agonize over his stolen pears. In Bruce's world, everyone is looking for the edge because in this game the percentage is always in favor of the house, and there's the ace of spades thrown down at the end and the game is over. In such a world, with death and dull audiences and dumb district attorneys, where the hype and the press release are gospel, where so much seems to depend upon luck, whom you follow on the playbill (whether it is Georgia Gibbs or the trained birds), whether you are the warden or Kiki, whether you are black or white, whether you have 29 cents for a glass of wine or you have to invent some pathetically transparent panhandle on the spot, when what you want most is nailed to the wheel of fortune and spun, round and round, where it stops nobody knows—in such a world, it is only the rube who does not restack the deck, reswitch the dice, find the angle.

For Bruce, hitting upon a stratagem does not involve any ethical issue, the old question about what it would take to make you kill or steal or sell your soul. This is not a Faustian problem. In the ludicrous context there is no issue about premeditation or of guilt. The stratagem arises spontaneously under great pressure and in response to overwhelming need. And it is this very irrationality and this total amorality that triggers our humor, for we all share to some extent Bruce's view of the world as a game weighted decidedly in favor of the house, or as a con, working to bilk us systematically of our deepest wishes, and we naturally rejoice to see the tables turned.

A misunderstanding, however, has arisen from the fact that the tables are sometimes turned by characters who do not appear to deserve our approbation. This raises what will turn into a perplexing question: whether Bruce should properly be called a satirist or a comedian. Indeed, if we feel contempt for characters like A.A. and Oral, who corrupt religion for their own selfish purposes, or the white party-goer for his racial prejudice, or even Frank Dell for his nationalistic slur, then we should be inclined to call Bruce a satirist. That this is a term which was commonly applied to Bruce, and which he himself came to use, ought not greatly to influence our judgment. In the first place, the term "satire" is frequently associated in the show-biz argot with any comedian whose material is only slightly more biting or personal than Jack Benny's. It is a code word, a convenience, with which managers prepare booking agents and MCs audiences for material that is just a little bit "different." But the term generally has no more technical validity in referring to genre than the word "epic" when it is applied to movies. It is true, for example, that Dick Gregory, who began as a comedian, became a satirist. He also got fewer laughs and less bookings. It would be a very unusual couple who would drop $100 at a nightclub to be satirized for living in an unintegrated neighborhood. Satirists are only incidentally funny, by choice, for they sense that the laugh unbarbs the anger. Lenny Bruce always tried to be funny. He was a humorist all his life. Sometimes he called himself a satirist, and not only because the word means the same as comedian in the show-biz language: he also assumed this title for the respectability and protection it seemed to offer his kind of humor.

Especially after the hostile audiences, the walkouts, the arrests, when Bruce was developing his new and shocking material on sexual and religious topics, he was pressured to find a justification for his act. Of course, this is a pointless task. Humor requires no other justification or defense than laughter. The trouble was that the ladies from the bus tour—two free tickets at an avant-garde nightclub—did not laugh. Neither presumably did Cardinal Spellman. Nor did the police. D.A. Frank Hogan of New York City was not especially known for his sense of humor. When Bruce had used the word "cocksucker" in his act and the police detective testified that Mr. Bruce recommended a sexual act prohibited by law, what could he say in his defense? That "cocksucker" can sometimes be a hilarious word? The detective had come into the nightclub, ordered a ginger ale, and sat through the whole show waiting for that word. He heard nothing else. Not only wasn't he amused, but presumably the word aroused his prurient interest, evidence necessary for the charge of obscenity.

Bruce, who was quickly becoming a legal expert of sorts in these matters, said what he thought was expedient to say. He came to claim first amendment rights of a satirist to criticize those very laws under which he was arrested. The obscenity law itself, the argument ran, gave an unnatural hypersexuality to words which people regularly use in their daily lives. This line of defense, which may have been relevant to the law, was utterly irrelevant to Bruce's act and to his art. It must have been an incredibly tense and enraging trial for Bruce to have sat through, while listening to lawyers' talk about his prurience. Nothing could have been further from the intention of his act than encouraging his audience to perform fellatio. Wouldn't they just let him do the act, the bit, in court so that they could see for themselves what he meant? No, they would not. They already had

his utterances, the evidence, in the transcripts. But they were misunderstanding it! Well, it wasn't a question of understanding; it was
a question of fact. Hadn't he in fact said . . . ? But for Bruce it *was*
a question of understanding and appreciation. Here he was called to
court with a judge in black robes and a legal secretary transcribing
it all for posterity, and they were missing the whole point! It must
have been intensely galling to an ambitious performer like Bruce, and
one so hungry for appreciation, to submit to such an important but
misguided examination.

Somewhere along the legal way, it must have occurred to him with
the brilliance of a vision that judges were not an audience, that the
courts were tied to The Law which spun out a whole system of its
own protocol and rationalizations. To paraphrase what he said about
wives hearing their husbands' confessions of adultery: "Courts have
no authority vested in them to hear any truth." So it must have come
almost with the force of a stratagem that he had to find the line that
would lead him safely through the labyrinth of the law. He must
have felt like Frank Dell, "punching, punching," looking for the
magic key. And suddenly, there it was. If he called himself a satirist,
a serious commentator rather than a comedian, he could say that he
was simply satirizing the laws under which he was arrested, claim
first amendment rights of free speech, and thereby politicize the trial
and set it upon a new and more defensible footing. In fact, this was
the line adopted in his most famous trial for obscenity in New York
against Frank Hogan. Bruce was able to enlist a great deal of literary
and political support. Much like one of his own comic characters, he
tried to snatch the con line even as he was sinking. And yet one
might wonder if ironically this solution was not almost as bad as the
problem. How much had it cost one so anxious for understanding
and appreciation as Bruce to deny his art?

We might consider for a moment this remarkable inequality with
which society treats the satirist and the comedian. We might well
wonder why Lenny Bruce, as satirist, had readily available to him a
whole set of prepared rationalizations that justified his art to society,
while Lenny Bruce, as comedian, had absolutely nothing in the social,
legal, or aesthetic tradition that he could appropriate to his defense.
All he could try to do, and it is noteworthy that he was consistently
prevented, was to plead for permission to perform his act before the

court to show how *funny* it was. Humor was no justification. But a satiric attack upon the law itself might be considered a possible defense. The natural conclusion to be drawn is that we prefer to be attacked seriously about topics that make us uncomfortable than to be made to laugh about the same material. This preference is most clear in the cases of satirists and comics employing equally objectionable material. (When they use milder stuff, they are rarely called upon by society to justify their practice.) Of course, this is not to say that satirists are never persecuted. In oppressive times they are nailed to the wall right next to the comedians. The point to be made is that in good or moderate times, when satirists and comedians employ the same objectionable material, the satirists stand a better chance of explaining their behavior with the ready-made justification provided by society.

Say a satirist and a comedian both use the word "cocksucker" with regard to an important person like the President. Let us assume that both artists perform their craft well, and let us further assume that both are arrested. The satirist in western civilization has in his favor a tradition thousands of years old which recognizes and places a unique value upon the concept of individuality. The principle of the privacy of conscience and opinion is recognized even and especially when it is abrogated. Moreover, the satirist labors within familiar boundaries: right and wrong, good and evil, sanity and madness. He works within these boundaries, and the intention and achievement of his art is the conveyance of a persuasive opinion. His goal is to portray his opinion both emotionally and intellectually so that the audience can at once feel and understand the significance of his thoughts. The audience, of course, is free to misunderstand him, or, if it conscientiously perceives his meaning, to disagree with him. After all, it's only his opinion. In any case, it knows how to cope with the situation because the problem of agreement and disagreement is an expected, familiar, and soluble phenomenon of everyday life. Thus, when the satirist in the example above is arrested, he immediately recognizes the role he must play. Instead of being put on the defensive by the arrest, he expresses outrage, moral indignation at the fascistic government which by his arrest has demonstrated its tyranny and which, after his acquittal, will be revealed as powerless. Numerous organizations which cannot approve of what he said will nevertheless rally in support of his right to say it. Advertisements will invite the public to come to his defense.

How entirely different is the situation of the comedian who is arrested for using the same material. Just try to explain a joke to the FBI or a judge. It won't work. The scene that one could imagine resembles the one described earlier in which Bruce portrayed an accident victim who unaccountably became aroused by the ambulance nurse:

> *Judge:* For the record, what exactly did you say?
> *Comic:* That the President was a cocksucker.
> *Judge:* How can you say a thing like that?!
> *Comic:* I dunno . . .
> *Judge:* Well, what did you mean by it?
> *Comic:* Nothing much. . . . I thought it would be funny.
> *Judge:* You thought it would be funny to call the President a . . . the word you used?
> *Comic:* It was a joke.
> *Judge:* Well, it wasn't funny.
> *Comic:* I guess not . . . I dunno . . .

It is impossible for a comedian to make a joke funny to someone by means of explanation, and it would be just as unreasonable to expect the comedian to know what his joke really means. The point is that the laughter of the comedian is a more mysterious response to the world than is the anger of the satirist. Most of us, and indeed most scholars of these two genres, offer more uniform and more confident opinions on satire than on comedy. It is this uncertainty about why we laugh that probably accounts for the difference we have been noticing in the way the world treats satirists and comedians, as well as for the fact that the satirist has at his disposal a much more clearly defined and socially respectable justification for his art than has the comedian.

Even if there is a tactical advantage in claiming the rights of the satirist, that does not prove that Lenny Bruce appropriated that title and those rights without, in fact, being a satirist. Most often, that title is associated with his skits on religion. We have seen in "Religions Inc." that the source of the humor springs from the deflection of our attention away from the serious religious questions of life, death, and salvation, towards the simpler question of how to turn a buck. If we were in the mood, we might become enraged at Oral's hypocrisy, and that would be a reaction appropriate to satire. But does Bruce's work actually put us in that mood? The fact that we laugh rather than become enraged suggests not. Rather than displaying anger and contempt, we are delighted with the brazenness with which the characters avoid the potential for fear in the religious subject matter. In effect, then, we identify with Oral rather than reject him as we would with satire.

After "Religions Inc." had gained its notoriety, Bruce offered a retraction, or at least an explanation. He said it was wrong to criticize the church's preoccupation with wealth and show. What had once seemed incongruous to him—the rich baroque cathedral in the midst of a ghetto—now made sense when seen from the poor man's point of view: "A raggedy-ass guy won't go into a raggedy-ass temple: 'I'm livin' in a shithouse—what I got to go in one for?'" So no one wants to take religion seriously, spiritually—neither the priests nor the parishioners. Bruce had a quick bit about a missionary and a savage:

Savage: Well, are you God?
Missionary: (*heavy brogue*) Well no, but, uh . . . heh, heh . . . What the
    hell, you know . . . just, uh . . . well never mind that . . . and, uh
    . . . I can do you a favor, you do me a favor—that's all.

The problem of religion and of the church is that we do not tend to believe what we cannot see. So anything that will make us believe is useful and acceptable. Now, is the missionary a bad man because he let the savage believe he was God? That could be the material of satire. But in this context, what we respond to in the missionary's "heh's" and "uh's" is the sudden mental calculation: "How disingenuously naive of the savage to think I'm God! And I do, in a way, represent God. And it would be hard to explain to this benighted fellow how I'm more different from God than like Him. And . . . heh, heh, what the hell." We do not laugh at this rationalization because it is evil, although in a different context, the context of satire, we might find it so. Rather, we laugh at the sudden revelation of the humanity of priests, how they must secretly long for that question to be asked. And really, we laugh at our own humanity, for are we not gods also? The priest's answer is yet another example of Bruce's characteristic interest in dramatizing the humor in the way the mind tries to cope with conflict and with reality. It is yet another version, though a mild one, of the stratagem.

Lenny Bruce's most outrageous portrait of priests is his millenial vision of Moses and Christ's unexpected and humorously unwanted return to earth at St. Patrick's Cathedral. What triggers the laughter is the fact that no one really wants them back. Moses, of course, is a Jew, and that's an embarrassment at St. Patrick's, and Christ, predictably enough for Him—but it is an incredible nuisance—is accompanied by a swarm of lepers. Cardinal Spellman, performing the Mass, is apprised of what is happening at the door of the church, but he tries to ignore it even as the disturbance grows into a commotion with the arrival of TV cameras and reporters. It is, after all, the Second Coming, and New Millenium or not, Chet Huntley has a deadline. Anyway, lepers are always good for thirty-second fillers. Finally, Cardinal Spellman pretends to welcome the lepers, but he warns them to stay in the back and not to touch anything, or leave anything, like arms or noses. Of course that is a terrible thing to say, but we are forced to identify with these sentiments in order to appreciate the humor.

The joke is told entirely from the point of view of Cardinal Spellman, that is, from the point of view of a priest who accepts Christianity but who finds Christ terribly inconvenient. Miracles, by definition, are hard to absorb on the spur of the moment. The clergy, instead of celebrating the event, treat it as if it were a catastrophe and Christ a nuisance. It is like a surprise investigation by the Board of Health. He could not have come at a worse time, and besides, He's interrupting the ceremony of the Mass. Doesn't He know He's in a church—bringing all those filthy lepers in there? The churchman's attitude releases our own mixed feelings towards Christ. Sure, He saved us, but He also established for our imitation an impossible model of self-sacrifice—washing dirty feet, loving the sick and the poor, turning the other cheek. This is admirable when it is done a couple thousand years ago and on someone else's property. Christ in the flesh is a different matter.

Part of our laughter comes from the surprise that Cardinal Spellman, of all people, would feel this way, and the laughter really springs from the recognition, experienced within the safety of the ludicrous context, that we feel this way too. It is perfectly all right for Christ to cure lepers as long as it happens far away from the public school, the house, and the nearby shopping mall and churches. As the white suburbanite said, "I got a sister. . . ." So what we are laughing at is the blatancy of the Cardinal's prejudice against Christ, and at his purely tactical rather than spiritual reaction to Christ's return: how can we get rid of Him with the least fuss? It is a pointedly practical and superficial answer to an incalculably profound religious event, the return of God to earth. We laugh at the superficiality because it is economical—it cuts the corner and avoids the really painful demands that true religion places upon the soul, and we also laugh because it reflects our own anger towards the ideal of Christian self-denial. Do we really want to die with Christ at Calvary?

Lenny Bruce, in another skit, portrays one of the thieves being dragged to the cross with Christ. A Brooklyn con-man voice keeps shouting for his lawyer: "Get my file down here! I'm in here for checks—how can I get crucified?" In the practical matter of life and death we are all prison lawyers. No one wants to suffer or die. In another bit, Bruce talks about the guilt that all Jews suffer for killing Christ no matter what the Ecumenical Council might be pressured into agreeing to say about Roman soldiers. Bruce cannot stand the tension and freely confesses: "All right. . . . Yes, we did it. I did it, my family. I found a note in my basement. It said: 'We killed him. Signed, Morty.'" The dynamics of all of these jokes depends upon the playful acceptance of duality and ambivalence.

Lenny Bruce's comedy makes us identify with Cardinal Spellman, with Oral, with the thief, with the guilt-ridden Jew. This is the method of comedy, inducing acceptance of others and ourselves through identification and empathy. The direction of satire is the opposite, towards rejection of others and ourselves. Both genres share the same content: human weaknesses. But one rejects them and the other embraces them in all their variety and ubiquity as the very trademarks of human nature. In this we see the crucial distinction between the satirist and the comedian. Both dramatize the discrepancy between what is and what ought to be. But the satirist rejects what is, and the comedian accepts it. Bruce shows us how characteristically human it is for us to raise ideals we cannot meet, and to hate, or at least subvert those ideals. His comedy trains us to accept our faults, our humanness. Some people admired or hated him for what they thought was his satire on Cardinal Spellman's religious hypocrisy. But what made Bruce really dangerous was that he made us agree with Cardinal Spellman that Christ was, in effect, a nuisance. A satirist would have made us hate Cardinal Spellman and ourselves. Lenny Bruce's comedy makes us enjoy and accept Cardinal Spellman and ourselves.

In all of his comedy, Bruce celebrates the infinitely varied and often surprising ways that human nature strives to subvert the human condition. And we can sense a lot about what that condition is like by the necessity of and the nature of the stratagems or means of subversion. In the jokes we have been examining, we saw Bruce concerned with such problems as the existence of God: "Ah, what the hell, you can think of me as God if it makes you feel better, heh, heh." Or the frustration of the need for love: "Screw the Irish!" Or the tension between the races: "That Joe Louis was a helluva fighter." Or the fear of death and the uncertainty of heaven: "We'll subdivide!" Or the desperation for oblivion: "I'm with the FBI. Buy me a drink." Or the unpredictable and personal nature of the sex drive: "It was the nurse's uniform." Gains in pleasure are won not only against the inhibitions and fears of the mind, but also against the intractable nature of the social environment and the physical world in which we live. According to Lenny Bruce, at least, the world seems not to have been designed for human happiness.

We can imagine how desperate the human condition appears to Lenny Bruce when we realize that any solution, any stratagem, no matter what it consists of, is acceptable and an occasion for rejoicing. We should observe the total lack of moral judgment here. We are not made to hate Oral even though he is a fraud, or Cardinal Spellman even though he is a hypocrite, or Frank Dell even though he is an ass, or the liberal white suburbanite even though he is a bigot, or the man at the bar even though he is an outrageous drunk, or the accident victim even though he has an erection in a disaster area. Moral judgment is left to the DA and to those who cannot laugh, who cannot see the joke for the content.

As I said earlier about the cosmic humor of a perfectly awful day, the comedy derives from an avoidance of the content, and rises to an aesthetic appreciation of the style or the context which seems to be imposed upon the contents. By almost any method of reckoning, a series of disasters such as Frank Dell suffered adds up to sheer hell. In only one very specious sense is the situation saved as an example of humor at work. And that is the sense that Bruce fastens upon. By the same account, one finds Bruce's characters in general sadly wanting, if not downright evil. But Bruce always discovers and shows us that one special sense in which they deserve our laughter and, as a prerequisite to laughter, our empathetic understanding.

The remarkable and dangerous aspect of Lenny Bruce's comedy is that he radically broadened the range of material that audiences had been accustomed to find humorous. If what we find funny is a measure of what is acceptably human, Lenny Bruce succeeded in broadening that definition, in making us more human. It was a door he held open into the darker areas of our minds and hearts. The light shone in for a time, and we laughed at more than we knew.

CHAPTER FIVE

Tristram Shandy:
A Comic Novel

EARLY IN *Tristram Shandy* the narrator begs his reader's indulgence. He must, he explains, tell his "story" in his "own way."[1] This is a request the reader must grant without reservation in order to enter into the book and to avoid being singled out for one of those embarrassing direct conversations with which Tristram surprises his less responsive readers.

Tristram's "way" is the salient feature of this comic novel. In Tristram's mind, the "way" is clearly differentiated from "story," that is, from plot line and content, so that when he begs to be allowed to arrange events and content in his own way, he indicates what is an obvious characteristic of this novel, the apparently irrational and unchronological sequencing of events which had originally occurred, as all events occur, in time. One of the special methods by which Tristram has made the "way" he tells his story his "own," that is, one of his true stylistic inventions, is this ripping of events from their logical relationship to neighboring events in the flow of time, and his presenting these events rather *as objects* which can be extracted and shown or only glimpsed before they are engulphed again by time. These events, as I shall show later, become in many ways like Hogarth's prints. Another analogy is a shoebox jumbled full of family photographs all out of order, but Grandma knows what each one is. "This is your mother when she was young, and this is your great uncle Herbert before he ran away to the gold rush in Alaska and we never saw him again, and this is you when you were born." Frozen in their amber light, the images live forever in a kind of idealized present, given coherence by the will and the personal experience of the narrator. It is the will of the narrator which keeps these events in a fictionalized present tense, keeps them from falling back into the unmarked, common grave of the past.

Tristram Shandy is an extreme example of the condition of all fiction as reminiscence—a conjunction of imagination and memory that recalls events to life as if they were present. This as-if-they-were-present, or hypothetical present, is sustained by the will of the narrator, and it is the particular and peculiar nature of narrative story-telling to achieve this fictive, or hypothetical presentness. I say hypothetical because narrative cannot achieve the true present any more than the true present can be isolated in reality. Even as Tristram tries to close with real time, he discovers that he can never reach the true present: "I shall never overtake myself" (IV.xiii.342). Narrative storytelling is an artful adaptation of the impossible human wish to keep the present, to make it reliable and repeatable—in short, to make it, the presentness of life (as it is not in reality) available and responsive to our wishes. Tristram has exaggerated the potential of fictional narration for the objectification and manipulation of present events—complicating, playing with, indeed, joking about the inevitable location of real events in real time.

Readers, of course, are familiar with consecutive narration as a means of representing the sequential, sometimes causal relationship of some events in time: "First . . . then . . . and then . . . and then. . . ." Almost equally commonplace is the narrative formula after the pattern of "Meanwhile, back at the ranch . . ."—a convention which allows a narrator to obtrude upon the linear consecutive format of the novel (novel time) an illusion of the complex contemporaneity of events in real time. But the issue of time in narration is extremely complex, involving many factors which a particular narrator may wish to emphasize or ignore. A number of different times relevant to *Tristram Shandy* may be identified briefly: (1) writing time (how long it took to compose the narrative); (2) reading time (how long it takes to read the narrative); (3) story time (the span of time—a day, a lifetime, three generations—that the narrative purports to cover); (4) digressive time (the span of digressive story time). There is also a factor of pace, that is, the ratio of reading time to story time. Especially important in *Tristram Shandy* is the issue of timing, the degree of incongruous juxtaposition between narrative elements. This is a topic worth a bit more investigation.

When comedians and tellers of jokes talk about the importance of timing, they refer to the fact that all narrative art is measured against and prized for its subtle variations from the tyranny of a standard, even a mechanically invariable rhythm of life. The incongruities so created, large and small, have their own effects depending upon the mental contexts in which they are received. For our purposes, what comedians call timing is a variation from standard rhythm which serves to call attention to an incongruity presented in a ludicrous context. This timing (actually a misnomer, for what we are considering is, in fact, a kind of mistiming, or at least a noticeable variation from what we would consider standard or normal timing) may be viewed as an incongruity itself. But, in general, timing helps to support the ludicrous context by alluding to the presence of a significant context.

It is worthwhile repeating a central idea of my first chapter: incongruities in timing, just like any other kind of incongruity, do not in themselves cause laughter unless they are presented in a functional ludicrous context. Bare incongruities of themselves are not funny. And in particular, incongruous variations in . . . . . . timing, as you have just experienced, do not necessarily cause laughter. They merely cause a wonderment about the intention behind the unusual emphasis. They simply point out the bare fact of a significant context and therefore are serviceable in calling or recalling attention to a present context or in cueing a change to a new one. The device of timing is used throughout *Tristram Shandy* to help establish and sustain the ludicrous context. At the level of the sentence, Sterne is a master of humorous phrasing. But timing, as we shall see, is also an inherent part of the structure of the novel.

Tristram Shandy, in narrating his story in his own way, plays with, indeed, parodies the novel's central preoccupation with time. For example, in narrating Dr. Slop's muddy encounter with Obadiah (II.viii.120), Tristram confronts the reader with the facts of reading time and story time—facts which usually enter the reader's mind subconsciously—and he exploits them for comic effect. Mrs. Shandy, it must be remembered, began her labor in I.xxi.70, when Uncle Toby rang the bell in order to send Obadiah for the man-midwife, Dr. Slop, whose arrival is signalled in II.vii.118 by "a Devil of a rap at the door." Patient Mrs. Shandy! Tolerant reader! Difficult labor as she underwent, it could not be as long as it would take the plodding reader to read until she finally was delivered of Tristram in III.xxiii. Tristram's "own way" of narration, of course, involves digressions which account for the vast difference between reading time and story time. However, at the beginning of II.viii, Tristram attempts to use the arrival of Dr. Slop to square and justify the incredibly wide ratio of reading time to story time by importing from theatrical criticism and preposterously forcing upon the novel a kind of unity of time principle: namely, that reading time must equal story time.

Tristram begins his humorous defense in this way: "It is about an hour and a half's tolerable good reading since my uncle *Toby* rung the bell, when *Obadiah* was order'd to saddle a horse, and go for Dr. *Slop* the man-midwife;—so that no one can say, with reason, that I have not allowed *Obadiah* time enough, poetically speaking, and considering the emergency too, both to go and come;—tho', morally and truly speaking, the man, perhaps, has scarce had time to get on his boots" (II.vii.119). Obadiah had enough reading time (i.e., "poetically speaking") to go and bring Dr. Slop back. However, if one disregarded all of Tristram's digressions and, in effect, timed only those few sentences after I.xxi relating to Mrs. Shandy's labor, the reading time, "morally and truly speaking," would be so short as to leave poor Obadiah, though morally and truly blameless, still in his socks.

Tristram then imagines a "hypercritick" who actually might disregard the reading time for all of the digresssions and thus calculate the story time for Mrs. Shandy's labor as "no more than two minutes, thirteen seconds, and three fifths." In response, Tristram disclaims all mechanical calculations and instead argues an impressionistic view of time, after Locke: namely, "that the idea of duration and of its simple modes, is got merely from the train and succession of our ideas" (II.viii.119). In this way, Tristram proposes to count the story time of his digressions towards the reader's impression of time passed, which comes to much more than the mere hour and a half of reading time with which he began his argument. Indeed, the story time in the digressions concerning Uncle Toby would come to four years, during which time Uncle Toby was recuperating from his war wound in London, "which must have prepared the reader's imagination for the enterance [sic] of Dr. *Slop* upon the stage" (II.viii.120). I suppose that if Obadiah were to be properly shod and Dr. Slop gotten, four years would be enough time for any narrator to accomplish the job if, that is, he wanted to. The reader of this novel knows by now that it does not really matter whether the time span is four years, one and a half hours, or only two minutes and some seconds. Tristram up until now has demonstrated an awareness of chronological verisimilitude only by radically departing from it.

From the beginning to the end Tristram asserted and occasionally defended, by further assertions or ludicrously exaggerated pleas and apologies, his own personal style of narration, his *"own way"* (IX.xxv.785). The time-frame arguments I have been considering in II.viii are read within the context of Tristram's own way, within the ludicrous context that envelopes the whole work. Irrationally, Tristram attempts to impose upon his narration a chronological verisimilitude. But equally irrationally he pins his defense upon a reading time of an hour and a half or a digressive story time of more than four years. It is, moreover, difficult to understand why and with whom he is arguing in the first place. Tristram entirely invents the "hypercritick" whom he makes insist that in order to avoid "a breach in the unity, or rather probability, of time" (II.viii.119), a narrator must make the reading time equal the story time. In fact, no such critic existed, and, as far as I can tell, while the topic of the unity or probability of time in the drama was debated upon many sides by every important literary critic in Restoration and eighteenth-century England, none of them attempted to carry this issue of a raging dramatic controversy into the area of fictional narration.

Tristram's creation of this imaginary controversy over narrative time serves several comic functions. It allows him to parody critical debate; to display, yet another time, the unique nature of his personality and "opinions"; and, most significantly for my discussion here, to indicate his awareness of the many modes of narrative time and their capacity for complex combination in the service of comedy. Readers, of course, know that Tristram is aware of his digressive nature, and it is also fairly obvious that this character trait is as much a part of his comedic personality as perplexed ratiocination is of his father's and military science is of his Uncle Toby's. Digressiveness is an emotional and mental hobby horse that Tristram, since he cannot dismount, rides with pleasure and only thinly disguised pride. His occasional apologies, like all those offered by characters about their hobby horses, are not serious. Tristram is never really sorry. His digressions, he knows, do not really need to be defended theoretically. His concocted arguments in II.viii and his fabrication of a critical debate make fun of writing by rules. But rules for temporal unity in the novel had never existed before Tristram made fun of them. So he invented the critical dogma that he makes fun of. Clearly, what he is not doing is reviving old satiric targets in the paper wars of dramatic criticism. What he is doing is, by intuition, and for the first time, defining and parodying the temporal nature of fictional narration.

The main feature of fictional narration that interests Tristram is its capacity to represent events, and often complex events, as they existed in time. As I have shown earlier, the complex temporal factors involved in fictional narration—reading time, story time, digressive story time, etc.—are subject to so many individual variations and combinations that story writers have an incredibly wide range of choices as to how to represent the relationship of events in time— from simple, sequential, chronological verisimilitude to the appearance of anarchy, where story time, digressive time, and reading time are so jumbled out of chronological order as to make it appear that the inexorable flow of real time does not exist. As I have suggested in my discussion of II.viii, Tristram's finding this side, and thereby discovering, virtually at the dawn of the genre, the phenomenally wide range of temporal representation inherent in the novel, is very much the result of his parodying the conventional narrative methods available to him, and reducing them to a radical absurdity. The seed of Tristram's style and much of the humor were planted and flourished in a mind driven by an irresistible impulse towards comic and sometimes grotesque mimicry.

Tristram states on the title page and argues in I.vi that his work is different from a typical novel, different from and more than a straightforwardly chronological account of his life. "I have undertaken," he warned his readers, "to write not only my life, but my opinions also" (I.vi.9). It would appear, however, that the fact of including "opinions" in a novel is not a strong enough idea to account for the kind of novel that Tristram has invented. It is important, therefore, to understand, especially since Tristram has provided enough information in this chapter, precisely what he meant by opinions and why he thought that their inclusion would change a novel enough to require the warning that he gives on the title page and more discursively here in I.vi. Tristram has already informed the reader under what circumstances and when he was conceived and also when he was born. But Tristram will not immediately satisfy the reader's curiosity with the promised information about "how" he was born because "Sir, as you and I are in a manner perfect strangers to each other, it would not have been proper to have let you into too many circumstances relating to myself all at once.—You must have a little patience. I have undertaken, you see, to write not only my life, but my opinions also."

Tristram, it is clear, will not provide the simple chronology of event that eighteenth-century readers expected would constitute the sinew of a novel. He bluntly informs the impatient reader that he cannot proceed more straightforwardly and expeditiously with the plot line, from how he was conceived to how he was born, because the reader and he "are in a manner perfect strangers to each other." The matter is, after all, tantalizingly intimate. But Tristram is also confident that "the slight acquaintance which is now beginning betwixt us, will grow into familiarity; and . . . will terminate in friendship." And "then nothing which has touched me will be thought trifling in its nature, or tedious in its telling." But in the very next sentence, Tristram happily salutes the reader as "my dear friend and companion" (I.vi.9). In one sentence we were "perfect strangers" and in the next we are dear friends. Tristram, as he wrote later, will not indulge "the vicious taste . . . of reading straight forwards" (I.xx.65). He may therefore have rather rushed his reader—"*O diem præclarum!*"—into the indulgence of dear friendship. Tristram's book certainly requires an exceptionally indulgent reader. Tristram knows that he has been "somewhat sparing of my narrative," so he now begs of his reader "to let me go on, and tell my story my own way" (i.vi.9). The emphasis, as Tristram places it, is upon "my own way" rather than upon "story," "my opinions" rather than "my narrative" and "my life." Tristram knows that he is writing a different kind of a novel.

In parodying the straightforwardly chronological novel, Tristram opens up the issue of time for conscious and self-conscious manipulation. Normally, conventional temporal formulas are used so as not to call attention to themselves as they expand or contract time within the narrative. As I said earlier, narrative has the capacity to represent the flow of events in real time, sharing the capacity of all art to improve upon reality by making it more available to our wish for pleasurable experience. So the reader accepts, in fact requires, excisions because it would be quite a nuisance to hear a story that took as long to tell as it took actually to happen. While all narrative, therefore, creates its own artful or idealized representation of actual time, Tristram goes an inspired leap beyond by making a comedy not only of conventional narrative representations of time, but of time itself. He can freeze time, make it an object, in effect make a fool of it, as when he stops time to describe Trim's tragically expressive hat in mid-fall, like the life of all men, and particularly poor Bobby, here now seemingly for an instant, and then, plop, "gone! in a moment" (V.vii.432); or when he stops Trim from reading Yorick's sermon just at the moment when Trim was "making a bow, and bespeaking attention with a slight movement of his right hand" (II.xvi.140). Tristram spends several pages minutely describing Trim's entire posture before he allows him to proceed. When Sterne said that he "would give both my Ears" for a Hogarth sketch, it was precisely this picture of Trim in this frozen moment that he hoped for and got.[2] In both printed page and ink on paper, time and the characters are trapped in lines of black, forever beginning to speak or beginning to hear.

If time can be stopped, objectified, and frozen by detail, it can also be split, atomized, infinitely divided. Poor Mrs. Shandy's labor is divided by parentheses hundreds of pages long, during which we are reminded of her existence and her plight only by the fact of her absence and by the occasional alarming sounds of running feet upstairs. Similarly, Tristram is accidentally circumcised in V.xvii.449 and is not permitted to scream until V.xxvi.457. Patient Uncle Toby is frozen in the middle of a sentence and in the act of knocking the ashes out of his pipe from I.xxi.70 until II.vi.114. If a moment can be lopped in half, the space between the halves can be filled, and filled, and filled with however many other moments Tristram wishes, an hour and a half's good reading time or four years of Uncle Toby's painful recuperation. The filling, moreover, need not consist of a digression containing a narration of consecutive events. No, indeed. It may contain its own split moments, and split, moreover, in such a way as not necessarily to reveal flashbacks but also flashes forward into the future. The temporal surface of the narrative may thereby become so warped back on itself and looped also into the future as to resemble in its incongruities a giddy carnival ride.

Tristram had been circumcised in V.xvii; he screamed nine chapters later; in the next volume, VI.iii, Dr. Slop attempts to apply a cataplasm to the wound but ends by flinging it in Susannah's face (496); VI.xiv carries the plot a week ahead when Mr. Shandy curses Dr. Slop for having maliciously exaggerated the report of Tristram's accident from a circumcision into a complete castration (520–21); the next six chapters (xv–xx.522–34) carry Tristram's life directly foward as Mr. and Mrs. Shandy debate in their *"beds of justice"* (xvii.524) and Mr. Shandy privately ruminates, philosophically, historically, and scholastically whether or not to put Tristram into breeches (xix.529–33).

What fills in the gaps? Part of it is narratively privileged information. For example, the gap between Tristram's accident and his scream is filled in with an explanation, after the fact, why the window, among other things, was not "well hung in our family" (V.xvii.449). Trim, it seems, had melted down the lead weights from the nursery window to make field pieces for Toby's sieges (xix.450–52). There is also the parlor talk while Tristram is being ministered to upstairs—Toby's military analogies (xx.452–xxiii.456)—interrupted by Tristram's defense of *"going backwards"* narratively (V.xxv.457). Yorick reads a chapter out of Rabelais (xxix.463–64). Mr. Shandy reads out of his manuscript *Tristrapædia* (xxxi.466–xliii.487). Tristram intrudes the whole story of Le Fever when Uncle Toby recommends Le Fever's son as a possible tutor for Tristram (VI.v.498–xiii.520). At VI.xx, Tristram breaks entirely with even the barest semblance of a sequential narration of the events of his life. "We are now going to enter upon a new scene of events":

> Leave we my mother . . .
> Leave we *Slop* . . .
> Leave we poor *Le Fever* . . .
> Let us leave, if possible, *myself*: —But 'tis impossible, —I must go along with you to the end of the work. (VI.xx.533–34)

The new scene is Uncle Toby's sham battles, ended by the Peace of Utrecht. But by chapter xxxiii, Tristram is again confused: "when a man is telling a story in the strange way I do mine, he is obliged continually to be going backwards and forwards to keep all tight together in the reader's fancy . . . and now, you see, I am lost myself!" (557–58). What Tristram wants to narrate is the love story of Toby and the widow Wadman, but it will require the digression of a whole volume before he will finally get to this matter again in the last volume.

The long digression that is volume VII jumps Tristram forward in time right up to the moment of his composition as, sick with a vile cough, he flies from Death into France, writing all the way. When he arrives at Auxerre, he tells us that he had been there before as a young man on his Grand Tour, accompanied by Mr. Shandy "with my uncle Toby, and Trim, and Obadiah, and indeed most of the family" (VII.xxvii.617). Tristram begins to recount an anecdote of that earlier trip and pauses to marvel at the incredible Chinese box of time-frames he has constructed: "Now this is the most puzzled skein of all—for . . . I have been getting forwards in two different journies together, and with the same dash of the pen—for I have got entirely out of Auxerre in this journey which I am writing now [the flight from Death], and I am got half way out of Auxerre in that which I shall write hereafter" (VII.xxviii.621), which is the full story of his Grand Tour as a young man, if he ever gets that far in the narration of the events of his "Life." He doesn't, for he left himself forever newly circumcised and about to be trousered in VI.xx.534.

Tristram pauses to admire the novelty of his narrative situation: "I am this moment walking across the market-place of Auxerre with my father and my uncle Toby, in [sic] our way back to dinner [on the Grand Tour]—and I am this moment also entering Lyons with my post-chaise broke into a thousand pieces [on his flight from Death] —and I am moreover this moment in a handsome pavillion built by Pringello [in Toulouse, where Sterne wrote this volume], upon the banks of the Garonne, which Mons. Sligniac has lent me, and where I now sit rhapsodizing all these affairs" (VII.xxviii.622). What a situation! This particular node of the narrative touches three places and three times: the literal present, as Tristram writes; the near past, during his flight from Death; and the far past, when he was on the Grand Tour as a young man. But all of these degrees of past time, in relation to the narrative of his life, which leaves off permanently when he is five years old, are really very far into the future.

For what purpose does Tristram bring these threads of time together and knot them here in this perplexity? In three places at three times, Tristram solves the dispersal of his personality with a punning punchline: "Let me collect myself, and pursue my journey" (VII.xxviii.622). Similarly, when he was earlier perplexed to account for Obadiah's return with Dr. Slop after "an hour and a half's tolerable good reading" time, or a hypercritic's mere two minutes or so direct story time, or Tristram's four years' worth of digressive story time, Tristram also ends this dispute with a punchline containing an extraordinary piece of privileged information. Four years would certainly have been enough time, one and a half hours would have sufficed as well, and even the hypercritic's two minutes, thirteen seconds, and three fifths would have been more than enough, for it turns out that "*Obadiah* had not got above threescore yards from the stable-yard before he met with Dr. *Slop*" (II.viii.119–20). So Tristram raised the problem of narration in order to reveal its complexities, and finally to make fun of it. And if a person, as the saying goes, can be of two minds, he can just as well be of three or more minds, and all thinking about different things, in different places, and different times. Tristram is portraying and taking comedic advantage of the condition of timelessness that prevails in fantasy. Time, for Tristram, can be the subject matter of comedy, but even more significantly, it can be the condition of comedy, a primary feature of the ludicrous context in which any subject of incongruity may be made humorous.

Time, for Tristram, is polymorphous. Like clay, it is a material that can be shaped for play, accepting whatever impression the artist wishes to give it, each impression by its destruction supplying the raw material for the next, unresisting in its malleability, uncaring of the successive contents imposed upon it, willing to be divided, and generous to each and every new image. Tristram parodies the "vicious" linearity (I.xx.65), the monotonous pulse of time and of discrete cause yielding discrete effect that conventional narrators and plodding "cabbage-planters" seek to imitate (VI.xl.572 and VIII.i.655).

Let me review the main characteristics of time as Tristram represents it. Time may be objectified, stopped at interesting moments; it may be split to allow other periods of time to intervene before the original time is resumed; it may be radically slowed or radically speeded up; it may merge and become one with several other times, so that a single narrative line may stand for several different times; it may go backwards. All narrative manipulates time in an artful way. But Tristram has invented new temporal formulas and pushed them to the extreme. He has, moreover, not disguised his technique; on the contrary, he has, as I have shown, gone out of his way to call attention to his manipulations; he has, as the Russian formalist critic, Victor Shklovski, so aptly put it, "bared the device."[3] Tristram's techniques are now familiar to anyone who is aware of these very same temporal manipulations that he regularly performs in his own fantasies. Time, in fantasies, is not a representation of real time in the real world. Rather, time functions in the service of wish and pleasure. In fantasy, time may be slowed, speeded up, divided to admit embellishments, run backward to provide happy causes for a pleasurable effect, repeated, etc. Unlike the inexorable regularity of time in the practical, real world, time in fantasy is infinitely plastic and receptive to every wish. So different from real time, this fantasy time is its opposite in characteristics, so much so that fantasy time is, in effect, timeless, a parody of the negative features of real time, inexorability, regularity, limitation, death. In fantasy, one may put his foot into the same spot in the same river as many times as he wishes without danger of the slightest prunelike wrinkle. Unlike the present in reality, which, even as it is about to be grasped, slips into the past, time in fantasy is willed by the dreamer into an idealized present which is always capable of complete and pleasurable manipulation.

I am now able to come to my main thesis, implied earlier, about the essentially comic nature of the narrative structure of *Tristram Shandy*. If, as I believe, the particular way in which a narrator represents events in time is of prime, and I would also say definitive, significance in distinguishing one kind of novel from another, I offer the following proposition: that Tristram's "own way" of narrating events and representing time functions primarily to support the ludicrous context which is the *sine qua non* of all works of comedy. As I have shown earlier, the ludicrous context in a work of comedy serves a corresponding ludicrous state of mind in the reader, which is characterized and defined by a willingness to apprehend the significance of a presented incongruity entirely for the purpose of pleasure and without regard to rationality, morality, and work.

The kind of time that Tristram attempts to represent is not the real time of the outer world, but that timeless time of mental consciousness where deepening degrees of pastness all can be called forth singly or in complex overlays into an idealized present which is susceptible of the radical temporal manipulations that I have just described. The context in the mind where this activity occurs is like a mental writers' colony to which memory and imagination retire to collaborate. This process can produce the kind of novel that represents what has come to be called a "stream of consciousness." Events are not narrated in a representation of real time, but in the idealized presentness of the mind's time, where idea succeeds idea, and one degree of past time precedes or succeeds another without regard to logic or the requirements of chronological verisimilitude. The attempt to portray or represent the flow of consciousness certainly has the potential for establishing the requirements of the ludicrous state of mind and of the ludicrous context in art, namely, irrationality, amorality, and an absence of work. But I hasten to warn that the ludicrous is only one of many other states that a representation of consciousness can effect with equal facility. That is to say, there is nothing essentially comical in the attempt to portray consciousness. The decisive factor is the intention of spirit and will to direct the flow of consciousness towards matters of incongruity which are experienced within a context of ludicrousness. "Stream of consciousness" refers to the attempt to represent the flow of ideas in the mind, but this is a term that, useful as it is, is still too general to define any specific genre. Tristram, for example, surely portrays the flow of ideas in his mind, but in particular, it is the flow of such ideas as pass through the ludicrous context of his mind. So it is a mind that is attuned first and foremost to incongruity experienced for the pleasure of laughter. And it is also a mind focused on the literary intention of recreating the incongruity and the conditions of its own laughter for the pleasure of readers.

Virtually everything that Tristram does with his text can profitably be regarded as a parody of conventional methods of narration. So far, I have been developing the argument that Tristram's manipulations of narrative time serve the ludicrous context where ideas and events which had originally been locked into a real historical and biographical chronology are here, within this privileged state, freed from the tyranny of real time and are juxtaposed primarily for the purpose of developing incongruities that yield mirth. The time that is represented in *Tristram Shandy* is the idealized present which is evoked in the service of the comic spirit. So what we have, chapter by chapter, is the reorganization of a past chronological reality into the idealized presentness of the comic vision, which reviews and recreates ideas and events for their value as incongruities that can satisfy the comic wish. Moreover, while time, the way Tristram uses it, is part of the general enabling ludicrous context, it is also very frequently itself a subject of the comedy, forming one pole for a great many incongruities. The first chapters of the book, for example, are entirely preoccupied with the subject of time, establishing the precise time and date when the sexual union of Mr. and Mrs. Shandy resulted in the conception of a being who would be born—and misnamed— two volumes later.

Tristram parodies conventional story time. Robinson Crusoe introduced the story of his *Life and Adventures* with a sentence that begins, "I was born in the Year 1632 . . ."[4] That sentence goes on to summarize, among other things, his father's life and career. By the third sentence, Robinson is already a young man about to rebel against the profession of law that his father had designed him for. Tristram's humorous point of departure has an even more narrowly literary point, as he rejects Horace's recommendation for beginning *in medias res* and not *ab ovo* (I.iv.5). Tristram will follow no man's rules. So he does not begin *in medias res*; he does not even begin with his birth; he begins with his egg!

If the reader imagines that Tristram's beginning here represents a devotion to his own idea of rigorous historicity, he is soon disillusioned by Tristram's practice. The narration of the events of Tristram's life is extremely slender and broken by digressions. Tristram knows that the "strange way" he tells his story keeps him "continually . . . going backwards and forwards" with the result that he is frequently lost himself (VI.xxxiii.557–58). Indeed, strictly speaking, he gets no further than his fifth year when he is about to be put into breeches in the middle of Volume VI. His flight from Death, which constitutes Volume VII, is a digression into the future, and the last volumes, VIII and IX, are a digression into the past to describe Uncle Toby's amours with the widow Wadman, four years before Tristram was conceived. So the novel ends before it began! Horace Walpole criticized this backwards direction in a way reminiscent of Dr. Johnson's characterization of a woman's preaching: "I can," wrote Walpole, "conceive a man saying that it would be droll to write a book in that manner, but have no notion of his persevering in executing it. It makes one smile two or three times at the beginning, but in recompense makes one yawn for two hours."[5] It should be apparent how widely Walpole missed the point of Sterne's extensive playfulness with time.

While time is used as a broad, general subject, one side of an incongruity the other side of which in Tristram's parodying style is conventional narrative time, time is also used throughout in narrower incongruities. In the very first chapter, a clock is associated with his conception and unhappily involved in the formation of Tristram's physical and mental being, perhaps even the course and destiny of his life. The clock is related to Tristram's wish to identify the beginning of his existence not with the date of his birth but with the date, even the hour, of his conception. Thus, he calculates, "I was begot in the night, betwixt the first *Sunday* and the first *Monday* in the month of *March*, in the year of our Lord one thousand seven hundred and eighteen. I am positive I was." Tristram can be positive because of his father's incredibly regular habits with regard to the time of sex:

> As a small specimen of this extreme exactness of his, to which he was in truth a slave,—he had made it a rule for many years of his life,—on the first *Sunday night* of every month throughout the whole year,—as certain as ever the *Sunday night* came,—to wind up a large house-clock which we had standing upon the back-stairs head, with his own hands:—And being somewhere between fifty and sixty years of age, at the time I have been speaking of,—he had likewise gradually brought some other little family concernments to the same period, in order, as he would often say to my uncle *Toby*, to get them all out of the way at one time, and be no more plagued and pester'd with them the rest of the month." (I.iv.6)

So the clock face becomes a lens through which can be focused at once Tristram's curiosity in the comical and his father's hobby-horsical obsession with philosophy as a means of regulating the body and its other passions. This "strange combination of ideas"—the clock and its incongruous connection with sex—also allows Tristram early to introduce the associationistic psychology of "the sagacious *Locke*" (I.iv.7) who supplied, but certainly did not recommend, a mental theory (or in this case, an *irrationale*, to coin a word) perfectly suited to the comic artist whose very purpose is to seek out those incongruities of idea and association that Locke condemned as unscientific and deranged.

Poor Mrs. Shandy, and, in consequence, the unborn Tristram fell victim to the absurdity of what to Mr. Shandy had seemed a very businesslike and reasonable association of the clock and sex, for from this "unhappy association of ideas which have no connection in nature, it so fell out at length, that my poor mother could never hear the said clock wound up,—but the thoughts of some other things unavoidably popp'd into her head,—*& vice versâ*" (I.iv.7). So it happened on the night in question, the night between the first Sunday and the first Monday of the month in which Tristram dates the beginning of his embryonic life, just at the moment when Mr. Shandy was about to fulfill that month's conjugal obligations, the unnatural but habitual association of clock = sex "unavoidably popp'd" into Mrs. Shandy's head as the *versa*, sex = clock, at precisely the most untimely moment: "*Pray, my dear*, quoth my mother, *have you not forgot to wind up the clock?—Good G*—! cried my father, making an exclamation, but taking care to moderate his voice at the same time,— *Did ever woman, since the creation of the world, interrupt a man with such a silly question?*" (I.i.2).

Thus it was that Tristram began his book with a complaint about the incongruity of his parents' behavior on the night of his conception: "I wish either my father or my mother, or indeed both of them, as they were in duty both equally bound to it, had minded what they were about when they begot me . . ." (I.i.1). It is a complaint, here and throughout, about the nature of creation, how absurdly it is entrusted to two beings of such inevitably different dispositions and interests and trains of association; how it falls prey to accident and the unconscious collision of ideas. It is a complaint about human psychology and human nature, how relentless and limiting are the processes of thought and feeling that generate the personality. It is a complaint about his very being, how it is called forth at the most inauspicious time, how by this first, he was doomed to other disastrous moments, badly born, nose crushed, misnamed, circumcised by a window sash, chased through France by Death, driven to write his life and opinions in his "own way," his style a welter of incon-

gruity and confusion, of false starts, interruptions, backtrackings—
a grotesque parody of that first, primal untimeliness and interruption.

Tristram begins his book in the language of complaint and he ends
it in the language of jest. "What is all this story about?" his mother
asked. "A COCK and a BULL," Yorick replied (IX.xxxiii.809). As Mr.
Shandy said, "Every thing in this world . . . is big with jest,—and
has wit in it, and instruction too,—if we can but find it out"
(V.xxxii.470). It is the finding it out that is the work of the comic
vision—the hard part, as it were. After reciting the sad story of Le
Fever's death, Tristram resumes his account of his own accidental
circumcision and of Dr. Slop's malicious rumor

that the nursery window had not only *   *   *   *   *   *
*   *   *   *   *   *   *   *   *   *   *   *   *
*   *   *   * ;—but that *   *   *   *   *   *   *   *
*   *   *   *   *   *   *   *   *   *   *   *   *
*   *   *   *   * 's also. (VI.xiv.521)

Between tears and anger, Tristram begins this chapter: "What a jovial
and a merry world would this be, may it please your worships, but
for that inextricable labyrinth of debts, cares, woes, want, grief, dis-
content, melancholy, large jointures, impositions, and lies!"
(VI.xiv.520). Most of Mr. Shandy's incredible, hobby-horsical theories—his theory of names, of noses, of the auxiliary verbs—most of
them, according to Tristram, "at first enter'd upon the footing of mere
whims, and of a *vive la Bagatelle*"—"beginning in jest,—but ending
in downright earnest" (I.xix.60–61). Mr. Shandy's method, turning
mirth into earnestness, is exactly the opposite of the comedian's de-
fiance of gravity. Tristram begins with complaint, with "this scurvy
and disasterous [sic] world of ours . . . this vile, dirty planet of ours"
(I.v.8), and he transforms the pain and the anger into mirth. The
difference between father and son on this point may be attributed to
temperament and personality, the difference in breed between the
philosophical and the comedic hobby horse. But there is involved
also an aspect of intention, choice, and will—a will to insist that in
whatever light the materials of experience may appear to others, to
the comedian they are made funny by the force of his comic vision.

In the dedication to William Pitt, added to the second edition of
Volumes I and II, Tristram wrote, and I emphasize the point of will-

fulness with my italics, "I live in a *constant endeavour* to fence against the infirmities of ill health, and other evils of life, by mirth; being firmly persuaded that every time a man smiles,—but much more so, when he laughs, that it adds something to this Fragment of Life." There is nothing that the comic spirit cannot make funny. This is not to say that all things are funny. All things mind their own business. Funniness and laughter are the result of a very specialized human perception—the perception of an incongruity within a ludicrous context. Within this special context, anything may be made incongruous and therefore funny. Thus, things which are not pleasant in experience can be made pleasant and funny by narration.

Tristram, needless to say, did not enjoy the sudden relationship between his sexual part and the window sash. When it happened, he did not wait nine chapters to scream (from V.xvii to xxvi). Such an encounter may be portrayed in any number of ways and have any number of consequences besides laughter. The pleasure in the event, as narrated, is entirely a product of the ludicrous context which tolerates, indeed encourages, any kind of manipulation of the content, no matter how irrational, immoral, or silly, so long as it results in the pleasure of laughter. When Tristram narrates that event in a ludicrous context, that is, when he wrote chapter xxvi of Volume V, he was a grown man. He had by then stopped screaming. And when he recreated the event within a ludicrous context, he could enjoy the manipulation of time and of cause and effect. He could also include details and an entire context that he could not have known or appreciated when he was five years old—the incongruous but characteristic way that his father deals with the event by rationalization; the way Dr. Slop has (to the delight of all who hear the rumor) exaggerated the accident into a total castration; and most of all, the set of seemingly discrete, self-contained causes and effects which incredibly combine to produce a unified system to deprive Tristram of his foreskin. For the sash which wounded him was no longer held by weights and pulleys. Trim had used them to make models of cannon for the fortifications and sham battles that alone kept Uncle Toby from dying of a wound which he also had received in the groin.

Time wounds. But if time also heals those wounds, it never quite effaces the shiny scar, and especially not the scar upon the memory, a reminder of one's vulnerability. Uncle Toby and Trim spend their mature life in obsessive reenactment of a past wound which still gapes in memory though the flesh has healed over. Wounds, great and small, preoccupy Tristram's consciousness. I now give a running account of the casualties, without regard for triage, as they occur in Tristram's narration. First, and apparently foremost in Tristram's mind is his botched conception, his first experience of the cruelty of time, wounded as he is by a clock (I.i.1–2). Even sperm cells, we learn, "may be injured" (I.ii.3). Helpful in dating this injury is his father's disability, his impotence, during December, January, and February 1717/18, because "he was all that time afflicted with a Sciatica" affecting his hip and thigh (I.iv.7). Impotence is the affliction, at one time or another, of all the Shandy men. Then, in I.xii, Yorick dies; his heart "was broke" (35). Later, Tristram plays with the idea of infant mortality, exaggerating the practice of intrauterine baptism with his own suggestion of intra-penile sperm baptism (I.xx.70). In the next chapter, Tristram refers to his Uncle Toby's war wound, "from a stone, broke off by a ball from the parapet of a horn-work at the siege of *Namur*, which struck full upon my uncle *Toby*'s groin" (I.xxi.75). Tristram raises the possibility of his own death in I.xxii, as he does often, when he promises to write as long as he is alive and well (82). As we find out, these are not hollow words, for Tristram's health does indeed deteriorate and, in the absence of a Xth volume, we presume him dead. Tristram ends the first volume with an account of his Uncle Toby's wound in the groin—the "bones were dismally crush'd." "He was four years totally confined," during which time he "suffer'd unspeakable miseries" (I.xxv.88).

Tristram opens the new volume with an account of Uncle Toby's convalescence and his "anguish" (II.i.96). Soon we hear that Toby's servant, Corporal Trim, is also "disabled," wounded "on his left knee by a musket-bullet, at the battle of *Landen*" (II.v.108). Next we learn that Mrs. Shandy in her labor "is taken very badly" (II.vi.114), an idea which Tristram plays with in the next chapter by describing Dr. Slop's knock on the door, which interrupted Mr. Shandy's train of thought, as having "crushed the head of as notable and curious a dissertation as ever was engendered in the womb of speculation" (II.vii.118). Mrs. Shandy, meanwhile, has her own problems. She cries out in II.xii.130. And we also learn that while Uncle Toby would "not hurt a hair" on the head of a fly, he would, however, at this crisis in Mrs. Shandy's labor, take the man-midwife off to a distracting tour of his model fortifications (II.xii.130–31). Below, in the parlor, Trim cannot finish his recitation of Yorick's sermon when he comes to the part about the Inquisition, for his brother Tom is still a prisoner of it in Portugal (II.xvii.161f.). Tristram ends this volume with an account of his father's fulminations against the irreparable mental injury caused "by the violent compression and crush which the head was to undergo" in the standard procedure of head-first delivery (II.xix.175).

By the ninth chapter of Volume III, "a sudden trampling in the room above" indicates that Mrs. Shandy's labor is reaching a crisis (197). In chapter x, there is more "trampling" (198) and then "a groan," and suddenly the Shandy household becomes a complete disaster area. Dr. Slop cuts his "thumb quite across to the very bone" (199). Mrs. Shandy, as Susannah reports, "is ready to faint," "the nurse has cut her arm . . . and the midwife has fallen backwards upon the edge of the fender, and bruised her hip as black as your hat" (III.xiii.216). Moreover, Dr. Slop, in demonstrating his method of forceps delivery, with the assistance of Uncle Toby, unfortunately "tore every bit of the skin quite off the back of both" of Toby's hands and "crush'd" all the knuckles "to a jelly" (III.xvi.220). As if the forceps were not as dangerous as they in fact proved to be to Tristram's nose, Dr. Slop raises the added threat of castration, "because, Sir, if the hip is mistaken for the head,—there is a possibility (if it is a boy) that the forceps * * * * * * * * * * * * * * *
* *"
(III.xvii.221).

Meanwhile, Tristram intrudes his "Author's PREFACE," in which he imagines his worst critics and himself so filled to the brim with full doses of wit and judgment that he grows rhapsodical at the thought and parodies a near-fatal vaporish fit: "but oh!—'tis too much,—I am sick,—I faint away deliciously at the thoughts of it!— 'tis more than nature can bear!—lay hold of me,—I am giddy,—I am stone blind,—I'm dying,—I am gone.—Help! Help! Help!" (III.229). But the moment of Tristram's birth is imminent: Trim enters carrying two mortars made from Mr. Shandy's mutilated jack-boots— "I have only cut off the tops, an' please your honour" (III.xxii.241–42)—

as well as the news that Dr. Slop is making a bridge, not, as Toby thought, for his fortifications (III.xxiii.243)—Trim had broken the old one with Mrs. Bridget underneath him (It was lucky "that the poor fellow did not break his leg.—Ay truly! my father would say,—a limb is soon broke, brother *Toby*, in such encounters" [III.xxiv.248])—no, it was a bridge for Tristram's nose which Slop's forceps have "crush'd . . . flat as a pancake to his face" (III.xxvii.253). So Tristram is badly born and wounded. All male Shandys are wounded or sciatic in the groin. For now it is only a nose, and Tristram warns his readers "to guard against the temptations and suggestions of the devil," for wherever the word "nose" occurs, "I declare, by that word I mean a Nose, and nothing more, or less" (III.xxxi.258).

To add insult to injury, Tristram, near death, "in a fit," and "black in the face," in the rush to baptise him, is misnamed (IV.xiv.343–44). Tristram goes on to narrate another genital wound—the idea, you see, preoccupies him—namely the suspicion Yorick fell under of purposely dropping a hot chestnut painfully into the "aperture of *Phutatorius's* breeches" (IV.xxvii.380). The end of this volume (IV.xxxi.399) and the beginning chapters of the next deal with the death of Tristram's older brother Bobby and with the way the news was received by the family. Amidst death, Tristram relates another curious, disappointing story of a botched birth concerning Mr. Shandy's "favourite little mare," which, instead of providing the fine horse which Mr. Shandy was already riding in his imagination, produced finally "nothing better than a mule" (V.iii.420). In the next chapter, sex and death are linked, as Mr. Shandy, in attempting to show how little the fact of death is feared, gives the example of Cornelius Gallus, the prætor, who died in the act of love: "He died, said my father, as * * * * * * * * * * * * * * * * * * *—And if it was with his wife, said my uncle *Toby*—there could be no hurt in it" (V.iv.426). This is also the volume for Tristram's accidental circumcision, which Trim describes with his usual expressiveness of gesture "by the help of his forefinger, laid flat upon the table, and the edge of his hand striking a-cross it at right angles" (V.xx.453).

In the sixth volume, Tristram mentions Trim's "lame knee (which sometimes gave him exquisite pain)" and goes on to start the sad story of Le Fever, ending in death (VI.vi.499ff.). Most curiously, an incidental detail of Le Fever's history reveals that his wife suffered the same fate as poor Cornelius Gallus: Le Fever mentioned that his "wife was most unfortunately killed with a musket shot, as she lay in my arms in my tent" (VI.vii.507). Uncle Toby observed later that Le Fever left out "a circumstance his modesty omitted" (508). The dangers of life are further elaborated by Dr. Slop's exaggeration of Tristram's circumcision (VI.xiv.520–21). Moreover, while Tristram narrates the sham battles that Uncle Toby and Trim fought year by year, in the middle of his apostrophe on the excellence of Trim's character, Tristram realizes that Trim is, in fact, dead: "But alas! alas! alas! . . . thou art gone;—thy genius fled up to the stars from whence it came;—and that warm heart of thine, with all its generous and open vessels, compressed into a *clod of the valley!*" And Tristram can scarce bear to imagine "that future and dreaded page" when he must describe Toby's funeral (VI.xxv.545). That page never comes. For Uncle Toby and Trim are long since dead already. But in accordance with his system of dialectics, Tristram ends this volume of death and disfigurement with the beginning of his account of Toby's love affair. However, Tristram's optimistic prediction in the last chapter of this volume, that "I shall be able to go on with my uncle *Toby*'s story, and my own, in a tolerable straight line" (VI.xl.570) was, by the same principle of dialectics, not to be fulfilled.

Death begins and dominates the seventh volume, moderated by a minor opposite theme of sex. In the very first chapter, "DEATH himself knocked at my door." But Tristram's good spirits invented a delaying stratagem: "ye bad him come again; and in so gay a tone of careless indifference, did ye do it, that he doubted of his commission— '—There must certainly be some mistake in this matter,' quoth he." Significantly, Death's appearance here interrupted Tristram in the middle of "a most tawdry" story "of a nun who fancied herself a shell-fish, and of a monk damn'd for eating a muscle." This is a paradigm of the style of Tristram's narration throughout and of the freedom with which unconscious association can find expression within the ludicrous context of the mind. Tristram decides to flee Death into France "whilst . . . these two spider legs of mine [the weak Shandy pins again!] . . . are able to support me" (VII.i.576–77). Immediately he is on the boat for Calais and "Sick! sick! sick! sick!

. . . O I am deadly sick!" (VII.ii.578). Soon, in Montreuil, an otherwise pitiful town, the dualism returns again in the "very handsome" person of the inn-keeper's daughter Janatone. Tristram's readers may study and measure at leisure the town's churches, "but he who would measure thee, Janatone, must do it now—thou carriest the principles of change within thy frame; and considering the chances of a transitory life, I would not answer for thee a moment . . ." (VII.ix.588–89). In chapter xii, Tristram asserts that he would prefer to die in an inn rather than at home to spare the attentive feelings of his friends, but not, he adds, shifting to humor, at the presumably horrid inn at Abbeville where he is now staying! (VII.xii.592).

Tristram introduces the image of painful limbs again in the story of the abbess of Andoüillets. We meet "a sciatical old nun" whose infirmity is ignored in preference to a "little novice" who is "troubled with a whitloe in her middle finger." And, of course, there is the abbess herself who had tried, without success, to cure the "stiff joint" in her knee by "touching it with all the reliques of the convent, principally with the thigh-bone of the man of Lystra, who had been impotent from his youth" (Vii.xxi.606–7). Tristram refers equally to Paul's miracle in curing the man of Lystra who was, in the King James version, "impotent in his feet" (Acts xiv.8), and to the vagaries of the sexual passion. Tristram treats the latter personally in chapter xxix: in demonstrating his ability to cope with and profit from the disasters of life by "making a penny of every one of 'em as they happen to me," Tristram calls upon his "dear Jenny" to "tell the world for me, how I behaved under one, the most oppressive of its kind which could befall me as a man, proud, as he ought to be, of his manhood—'Tis enough, said'st thou, coming close up to me, as I stood with my garters in my hand, reflecting upon what had *not* pass'd—'Tis enough, Tristram, and I am satisfied, said'st thou . . ." (VII.xxix.624).

The mischances of love are further exemplified in Tristram's determination, while in Lyons, to visit the (alas) nonexistent tomb of the two lovers, Amandus and Amanda, whose hapless career the infatuated Tristram narrates as a kind of perverse shaggy-dog story. The two lovers, cruelly parted, wander "round, and round, and round the world," until chance brings them together at the gate of their native Lyons, where

> each in well known accents calling out aloud.
> Is Amandus ⎫ still alive?
> Is my Amanda ⎰
> they fly into each others [sic] arms, and both drop
> down dead for joy. (VII.xxxi.628)

Then, Tristram, in sensitive communion with "the patient endurance of sufferings" (VII.xxxii.630) of a "poor ass" (629), unfortunately is inflicted with an injury from the beast's pannier to his "breeches pocket," gashing it "in the most disasterous [sic] direction you can imagine" (632). It could have been much worse. Meanwhile, Tristram continues his flight from Death: "Still he followed,—and still I fled him" (VII.xlii.645) until, on the rich plains of Languedoc, he almost tarried to dance forever with the beautiful Nannette to the music of pipe and tabourin played by a youth who suffered from—what else?—of course, from lameness (VII.xliii.650). Thus ends the seventh volume, with the ideas of love and lameness providing a transition to the love affair that the afflicted Toby conducted with the widow Wadman.

In chapter v of Volume VIII, Tristram asserts that both "ancient and modern physiologists" fully understand the reasons why "a man with a pined leg," so long as it proceded "from some ailment in the *foot*" (Toby's, however, was affected by an injury to his groin), "should ever have had some tender nymph breaking her heart in secret" for him (VIII.v.660). Tristram keeps up the dialectic of pleasure and pain: he comments that he is still "tormented with the vile asthma" he got "in skating against the wind in Flanders," which had its effect on a recent ambivalent event, for he had broken a vessel in his lungs and lost two quarts of blood after "a fit of laughter, on seeing a cardinal make water like a quirister (with both hands)" (VIII.vi.663). Pain from pleasure; pleasure from pain. It is the ironical dialectic.

As Trim said, introducing the story of his love affair with his nurse, if he had not in fact been wounded, "if it had not been for that single shot, I had never . . . been in love" (VIII.xix.693). Meanwhile, Trim and Toby debate which injury causes more anguish, one to the knee or one to the groin, while Mrs. Wadman eavesdrops with evident interest (VIII.xix.695). She launches her attack upon Toby with her own, albeit dissembled, injury: "a mote—or sand—or something—I know not what, has got into this eye of mine—do look into it . . ." (VIII.xxiv.705). It was a glancing wound, but "it had gone to his heart" (VIII.xxvi.710). It remains only for Mrs. Wadman to discover the extent of the wound—not the one on his heart, but the other, as she calls it, "the monstrous wound upon his groin" (VIII.xxviii.713).

In the ninth and final volume, Tristram is involved in the completion of the story of Toby's amours. But he is also aware of his own illness, the approach of Death, and the final separation from his own beloved Jenny. He must rush to complete his book. So for once, he will not digress into an argument:

> I will not argue the matter: Time wastes too fast: every letter I trace tells me with what rapidity Life follows my pen; the days and hours of it, more precious, my dear Jenny! than the rubies about they neck, are flying over our heads like light clouds of a windy day, never to return more—every thing presses on—whilst thou art twisting that lock,—see! it grows grey; and every time I kiss thy hand to bid adieu, and every absence which follows it, are preludes to that eternal separation which we are shortly to make.—
> —Heaven have mercy upon us both! (IX.viii.754)

At the beginning of chapter xxiv, Tristram lost "some fourscore ounces of blood" (IX.xxiv.779). In this chapter, he takes us back to his flight from Death, which was the subject of the last volume. As he continues his flight, he introduces us to poor Maria, wounded into pathetic insanity by disappointed love. It is a tender moment. "I rose up, and with broken and irregular steps walk'd softly to my chaise.—What an excellent inn at Moulins!" (IX.xxiv.784).

Tristram hastens to the long-postponed joke which concludes the story of Toby's amours. It turns on the natural curiosity of Mrs. Wadman, "whose first husband was all his time afflicted with a Sciatica"—is no man whole and hale?!—"to wish to know how far from the hip to the groin" (IX.xxvi.791), that is, precisely, as she finally had to ask Toby directly, precisely "whereabouts . . . did you receive this sad blow?" No problem. Toby simply dispatched Trim for the "large map of the town and citadel of Namur and its environs," on which he "measured off thirty toises, with Mrs. Wadman's scissars [sic], from the returning angle before the gate of St. Nicolas," and immediately he "laid her finger upon the place" where he was injured (IX.xxvi.793–94). As if this mischance were not enough—and for Tristram when was once enough?—he ends this volume and the work with another vagary of the love instinct.

Obadiah, whose wife had just been delivered of a boy, was awaiting, without result, a similar performance by his cow which had been serviced by Mr. Shandy's bull. Obadiah may have long to wait, as he complains that "most of the townsmen . . . believe that 'tis all the Bull's fault" (IX.xxxiii.808). Mr. Shandy had just been inveighing philosophically against "lust," the "unruly appetite" (IX.xxxii.805), and now comes the charge of impotence. Untimely innuendo! The poor man defends himself against Obadiah with a jest very much in bad taste, by impugning Obadiah's own potency and the legitimacy of the child. Hearing that Obadiah's infant has a great deal of hair, Mr. Shandy insists that "this poor Bull of mine . . . is as good a Bull as ever p–ss'd," and "had he but two legs less," the beast might have been accused of the other birth, and as a correspondent in the divorce, been "driven into Doctors Commons and lost his character" (IX.xxxiii.808).

So the novel has turned full circle. It began and now ends with a botched conception, with Mrs. Shandy's "unseasonable question" (I.ii.2) and with Uncle Toby's unresponsive answer. It opened with the beginning of Tristram's life and ended with the presumption of his death. It began with an interruption of Mr. Shandy's potency and ended with a prevarication about the potency of Uncle Toby, and the reasonable certainty, despite Mr. Shandy's rude joke, about the sterility of his bull. Obadiah's wife has just given birth to a son, but his cow remains empty. It began in the language of complaint and it ends in the language of Yorick's jest: it is all a cock and bull story. It began with new life, and it ended—since there is no tenth volume and Tristram had often said that he would write as long as he lived—with death. The narration began with Tristram's conception in the year 1718, and it ended with Uncle Toby's amours in the year 1714. But going backwards in the privileged world of the memory where time exists in the ideal present—going backwards in the memory could not stop the inexorably mechanical forward progress of the real world's clock, and in the end, Tristram lies dead and buried in the space that would have been occupied by the tenth volume. It is a space very much like, but far more expressive in its infinite vacancy than the two black pages Tristram provided for the accommodation of the sad feelings upon Yorick's death (I.xii.37–38).

Alas, poor TRISTRAM!

And surely there is a sadness to be felt there. But it is a sadness that is complicated by being one side of an incongruity. The other side is Tristram's joking conclusion to Volume IX and his playfulness with time throughout. We have been driven forwards and backwards in time by the vagaries of Tristram's stream of comic consciousness, so that we do not well know where we are except in the constant presence of his comic good spirits, which never, even when Death knocked, failed him.

In summarizing the wounds and injuries of various sorts to be found in this novel, I hope I have indulged the reader's pleasure in recalling the work. And if this selective collation sounds rather like a summary of the entire novel, the critic is bound to ask questions. Why, for example, did Tristram choose the wound, in all its major and minor variations, as the central image of his work? By what means did he generate incongruities with this image? And in what ways did he characterize the ludicrous context which houses these incongruities?

From conception to the grave, even a fortunate life is beset with "pitiful misadventures and cross accidents" (I.v.9). As Tristram describes it, life is a series of accidents and mischances. His mother's previous false pregnancy had ventured his nose under the cruel forceps of Dr. Slop whose cut thumb and vexatious spirit transformed the device into an engine of destruction. And if it is bad luck not to have a chamber pot nearby, it is more than double bad luck not to have weights and pulleys in the window sash. And while poor Uncle Toby, like every soldier, stood a risk of injury at the siege of Namur, it was a stroke of painful and near fatal mischance that it was his groin that happend to be "in one of the traverses, about thirty toises from the returning angle of the trench, opposite to the salient angle of the demi-bastion of *St. Roch*" (II.i.96). And with regard to Tristram again, if he is even the slightest bit right that his interrupted conception had even the smallest effect upon his later life, it was indeed a piece of ill fortune that his father's extreme devotion to regularity had cemented the association of sex and the clock so inevitably in Mrs. Shandy's mind as to prompt her interruptory fateful question. And if Mr. Shandy were not so devoted to philosophical speculation as his way of attempting to insure a perfect security over the accidents of life, in particular, if he had not developed his theory of names as a means of guaranteeing the good character of his new-born son, he would not have insisted upon the name Trismegistus, a name too easily lost and botched in the memory of anyone, and especially in the haste of the overwrought and normally scatter-brained maid, Susannah. And of course, if Uncle Toby had not been as obsessive about his sham battles as Mr. Shandy was about philosophical order, the lead weights and the pulleys would not have been fabricated into toy cannon, and Tristram and his bedroom window would have remained "well hung." And if Uncle Toby had not saved his life by his obsessive reenactment of and devotion to the military history of his own wound, so much so that it became his hobby horse, he might have been able to understand Mrs. Wadman's question in the spirit in which it was asked, and not as an inquiry into military cartography, and thus would have rescued the teetering affair from the debacle of misunderstanding and cross purposes into which it fell.

Wound, injury, accident, and error abound in this novel. But these are never simple fractures. Their etiology is extremely, incongruously complex. The ways characters are, their very individuality, their unique cast of mind and mental process, as opposite and far apart as they usually are, sometimes surprisingly converge in a complex nexus of disastrous incongruity. As Tristram observed,

> Though in one sense, our family was certainly a simple machine, as it consisted of a few wheels; yet there was thus much to be said for it, that these wheels were set in motion by so many different springs, and acted one upon the other from such a variety of strange principles and impulses,—that though it was a simple machine, it had all the honour and advantages of a complex one,—and a number of as odd movements within it, as ever were beheld in the inside of a *Dutch* silk-mill. (V.vi.427)

As a crude comparison, imagine a pedestrian in a Keystone comedy being crashed upon the head by a piano, albeit a balsa prop. The movers in the apartment high above were extremely ill-adroit in their handling of the winch. But our laughter would be intensified and complicated if we knew that the pedestrian were genetically prone to accidents, had, in fact, just emerged from the manhole into which he had fallen, and that the accident was not due to clumsy movers but to the little rich boy in the penthouse above who had abruptly ended his lesson in a piano-pushing tantrum.

Tristram is hardly conscious of what may be called simple natural accidents, the hammered thumb, the spilt milk. But he is entirely devoted to and preoccupied by the kind of "cross-accidents," as he calls them, created by the collision of two beings so far apart and so discretely alone in their separate personalities, thought processes, and intentions that it would be more surprising for them to come near each other, much less actually collide. But Tristram draws the vectors of their personalities and extends them infinitely so that at some point they do converge—not in the real world, surely, but in the privileged world of comedy. It is important to observe that these collisions of personality and the pain, great or trifling, that they cause, are not intentional. This is not a satire on human nature. When two creatures are so totally self-absorbed and alone in the private pleasure of furiously riding their separate hobby horses, the last thing they imagine or wish is a collision at a sudden and unforseen turning in the lane. Indeed, the crucial word is aloneness.

The ground upon which Tristram paints his eccentric portrait is the aloneness, the separateness of the mind. The picture that Tristram finally paints is one of the mind's ceaseless activity. And if there are not things in the real world that insist upon consideration, the mind will think of itself. For there is always the unknown, subterranean, silent sea on whose secret tides swim schools of ideas, peaceful, pleasurable, freakish, or predatory, that never see the light of consciousness. In describing Dr. Slop's silent wish that Mrs. Shandy's already painful labor might be further prolonged until he could untie the devilishly tight knots in his obstetrical bag and so earn his fee, Tristram observes that "the thought floated only in Dr. *Slop*'s mind, without sail or ballast to it, as a simple proposition; millions of which, as your worship knows, are every day swiming [sic] quietly in the middle of the thin juice of a man's understanding, without being carried backwards or forwards, till some little gusts of passion or interest drive them to one side" (III.ix.197).

Following Hobbes and Locke, Tristram portrays the generation of the personality as a mechanical process of association which, beginning in accident, becomes the habitual mode of thought. Tristram attributed his irregular personality to the accidentally irregular motion imparted to his "animal spirits" (I.i.1) at the moment of his accidentally interrupted conception, so that whatever "tracks and trains" they fall into, "when they are once set a-going, whether right or wrong, 'tis not a halfpenny matter,—away they go cluttering like hey-go-mad; and by treading the same steps over and over again, they presently make a road of it, as plain and as smooth as a garden-walk, which, when they are once used to, the Devil himself sometimes shall not be able to drive them off it" (I.i.2). Moreover, the trains of association of ideas and early impressions are so strong as to set the fate of the personality into a fixed individuality, into such an idiosyncratic system of thought process and verbal reference, that his very being, his every attempt to express himself and to communicate his being, incongruously and ironically isolates him deeper within the prison of his own being.

Tristram fully understands the dilemma embodied in the very idea of individuality, for the unique process of consciousness that makes a being an individual also separates him from his brothers, makes him alone, and dooms him to be misunderstood. And in this formulation, the more forceful and distinct the individual consciousness, the more he is doomed to loneliness and to misunderstanding. What Tristram says of his father's characteristic process of consciousness, his devotion to philosophical oratory, may be said of Tristram himself, and of all the characters in this book: "it was indeed his strength—and his weakness too" (V.iii.419). This is not just a rehashing of the comedy of humors to be found in Jonson's plays and later in Restoration comedies. Tristram does not just laugh at his characters' obsessions and monomanias. There is a profound sympathy in his comic characterizations. Tristram understands that the very act of being is an incongruity. For in being ourselves we are doing what everyone else is doing, yet we are like none of them. In solving the enigma of being, we become ourselves enigmatic.

The matter of Uncle Toby's life, like all of the matter in this book, is capable of being viewed in any number of different lights. The remarkable force in this book is Tristram's comic vision, which makes us see everything within a ludicrous context, as part not only of the human comedy but the comedy of being human. As a schoolboy, young Toby's heart beat to the drums of war, he said, in an attempt to justify his life: "was it my fault?—Did I plant the propensity there?—did I sound the alarm within, or Nature?" (VI.xxxii.555). And whose fault was it that Uncle Toby was standing in one of the traverses "thirty toises from the returning angle of the trench, opposite to the salient angle of the demi-bastion of *St. Roch*" (II.i.96)? And why not only twenty toises? It might have been worse. And why had he not been a cobbler? Anthony Ashley Cooper, the third Earl of Shaftesbury, understood the problem when he elaborated on Socrates' great motto: know thyself.

There is more than one inhabitant in each body, and our obligation, according to Shaftesbury, is to become acquainted with our various inner voices. "As cruel a court as the Inquisition appears," wrote Shaftesbury, "there must, it seems, be full as formidable a one erected in ourselves, if we would pretend to that uniformity of opinion which is necessary to hold us to one will, and preserve us in the same mind from one day to another. Philosophy, at this rate, will be thought perhaps little better than persecution." In order to avoid the imputation of a tyrannical dogmatism, Shaftesbury recommends a complete self-examination, "when by a certain powerful figure of inward rhetoric the mind apostrophises its own fancies, raises them in their proper shapes and personages, and addresses them familiarly, without the least ceremony or respect." The object of this operation is to develop an informed will and to assure the individual of "a certain resolution, by which he shall know where to find himself; be sure of his own meaning and design."[6]

Tristram, however, portrays a mechanical interpretation of character in which the self is immutable. In Tristram's characterizations, one finds out what his self is, accommodates to it, and enjoys it as much as possible, even though it makes him a fool, for his strength is also his greatest weakness. So Mr. Shandy is a dupe to philosophical rhetoric; Mrs. Shandy is a dupe to feminine pride; and Tristram is a dupe to his own sense of humor, of his telling his story in his own way, of his trifling on the road, of his donning the fool's cap with a bell on it.

Meanwhile, Uncle Toby lies wounded in the groin, the "bones

. . . dismally crush'd," suffering "unspeakable miseries" while he was convalescing "four years totally confined," and, except for one outburst, patiently submitting to his surgeon's course of treatment that in all that time made him no better. His only pleasure was in recounting the history of his wound with all of the military details and terminology, upon the principle that "the history of a soldier's wound beguiles the pain of it" (I.xxv.88). And yet, cruel dialectic, the pleasure that he got in the telling was much overbalanced by the pain, the "sharp paroxisms and exacerbations of his wound" (II.i.95) which "arose out of the almost insurmountable difficulties he found in telling his story intelligibly, and giving such clear ideas of the differences and distinctions between the scarp and counterscarp,—the glacis and covered way,—the half-moon and ravelin,—as to make his company fully comprehend where and what he was about" (94). Unless he had hit upon the expedient of "a large map of the fortifications of the town and citadel of *Namur*" (96), the perplexities of his mind, communicating themselves to his wound, "would have laid him in his grave" (I.xxv.89). So because Uncle Toby could not precisely explain, and his guests could not precisely understand what, for example, a gazon was—what precisely *is* a gazon?—he would, except for the happy expedient of the map, have perished a martyr to Locke's theory that a great deal of the world's confusion results from "the unsteady uses of words" (II.ii.100). Poor Uncle Toby, "his life was put in jeopardy by words" (101).

The material of this episode, like the matter throughout this work, is subject to as many different modes of expression as there are feelings in human nature. Quite simply, a warrior is injured. His long and painful convalescence is rendered precarious by his emotional shock which continues long after the time of the injury. He remains confused and confuses others, until he discovers the device of the map and ultimately his model fortifications, which enables him at once to account for his wound and to turn the painful event into the pleasure of a totally self-absorbing hobby. It certainly may be true, as Tristram said, that "the history of a soldier's wound"—or anyone's wound, appendectomy, car accident, tax audit—"beguiles the pain of it" (I.xxv.88). Tristram too must communicate the wounds and pains of his own life or equally suffer the even more excruciating torture of suffering privately. Tristram's *Life and Opinions* is very much like Uncle Toby's fortifications—an attempt to cope with life by representing it. We find ways of accommodating ourselves to shocks by narrating them, manipulating the details and the context, even if only to ourselves in our own memory, as a means of accepting, or gaining a kind of pleasure from and power over, events in our own history which at the time may have rendered us speechless with the shock of the pain and humiliation.

It is one thing to accommodate ourselves to the past by representing it. It is another to make, as did Uncle Toby, a fortress prison of it. In anything but the tolerant comic light in which Tristram views his uncle, Toby might be seen as a lunatic, perhaps even a criminal lunatic. He had incited Trim to chop out all the lead gutters in the parish church, as well as the lead weights of the window sash which resulted in the dreadful accident that befell young Tristram. But in the all-forgiving, all-tolerating ludicrous context, incongruous behavior, indeed all incongruity, is not only accepted, it is turned into joy. While the spectacle of a grown man spending his life playing with mud-pie castles is tinged with the pathos of psychopathology, it is also and more importantly a celebration of the joy of existence, the miracle of pleasure out of pain. Only a sadist would attempt to upset the possibly lunatic balance which gave pleasure to and preserved the health of Uncle Toby's broken body. Tristram's comic spirit celebrates whatever individual solution allows us to persevere in and to extract a pittance of pleasure from "this scurvy and disasterous [sic] world of ours" (I.v.8).

Everyone's personality is an idiosyncratic solution to the problem of existing in and finding pleasure in this world. Here is matter enough for incongruity. Each character has his own hobby-horse. While everyone's problems are more or less the same, accident, confusion, injury, pain, and death, each one rides through these problems on his own peculiar steed. Seen from the context of ludicrousness established by Tristram, the very fact of the existence of individual personalities is humorous. The personality becomes one side of an incongruity, an eccentric adaptation to the universal problem of existence. The irrational and amoral aspect of the ludicrous context frees us from the necessity or even the temptation of making any judgments concerning the moral or practical value of these adaptations. For example, only the worst kind of spoilsport would observe that Uncle Toby is certifiably psychotic and makes no regular contribution to the world. While he does display compassion for Le Fever and his orphan, he also squanders his pension and any other money he can beg or borrow in order to sustain his extravagant, miniaturized fantasy world of toy soldiers and mud fortresses. He is so preoccupied with this fantasy that he is virtually incapable of conducting a rational dialogue with any other human being but his servant Trim, who shares and encourages this withdrawal into fantasy. But if the way that Toby has reacted to the pain of life by withdrawing into himself renders him lonely and misunderstood and misunderstanding even and especially when he is attempting to converse and to understand and to be understood, his situation—it cannot really be called a true predicament in this comic context—is shared by virtually every important character in the novel.

Mr. Shandy is so absorbed in philosophical speculation that even as he was composing his treatise on the education of his son, his *Tristra-pædia*, it did not seem to trouble him that his child was growing apace and thereby superseding the work in progress so that "every day a page or two became of no consequence." Mr. Shandy, of course, vastly enjoyed treatises, but for Tristram, "the misfortune was, that I was all that time totally neglected, and abandoned to my mother" (V.xvi.448). And Mrs. Shandy, except for a really very slight stubborness over the selection of a midwife (which was actually a stubbornly complete acquiescence to Mr. Shandy's stipulation in the marriage settlement)—Mrs. Shandy confronts the world and her husband, or more precisely withdraws from them both behind a beatific smile of abject complacency. A delightfully comic example of this confrontation is the *"beds of justice"* (VI.xvii.524) which Mr. Shandy used to attempt to engage his wife, naturally without success, in debate over matters that concerned the family. It is enjoyable to recall just a short part of this comical *pas de deux*:

> We should begin, said my father, turning himself half round in bed, and shifting his pillow a little towards my mother's, as he opened the debate—We should begin to think, Mrs. *Shandy*, of putting this boy into breeches.—
>
> We should so,—said my mother.—We defer it, my dear, quoth my father, shamefully.—
>
> I think we do, Mr. *Shandy*,—said my mother.

—Not but the child looks extremely well, said my father, in his vests and tunicks.—

—He does look very well in them,—replied my mother.—

—And for that reason it would be almost a sin, added my father, to take him out of 'em.—

—It would so,—said my mother:—But indeed he is growing a very tall lad,—rejoin'd my father.

—He is very tall for his age, indeed,—said my mother.—

—I can not (making two syllables of it) imagine, quoth my father, who the duce he takes after.—

I cannot conceive, for my life,—said my mother.—

Humph!—said my father.

(The dialogue ceased for a moment.)

—I am very short myself,—continued my father, gravely.

You are very short, Mr. *Shandy*,—said my mother. (VI.xviii.526–27)

What a couple! Mr. Shandy had pursued the issue of his height from a genetic point of view. How exasperating not only to have the scientific context of one's admission of shortness ignored, but also to have the admission agreed to as a matter of simple fact.

In what context did his wife so promptly agree that he was very short? It might be a pointless context, like her other replies. There might be some criticism in her agreement: perhaps he was not just very short in a relative sense, in comparison to the projected growth of his young son, but too short in an absolute sense. The word may also refer obliquely to another embarrassment, the extreme shortness of noses in the Shandy family history (III.xxxii.259). And the train of association may easily be carried further to a more private anxiety especially since this bed of justice, Tristram tells us even as he modestly draws the curtain on this scene, was conducted on "the first *Sunday* night in the month" (VI. xvii.523–24; xviii.529). Mr. Shandy has already wound the clock. We are not told the state of his sciatic hip. But we do remember that on such a night as this, if Mrs. Shandy was capable of an unseasonable question, she may also be capable of an unseasonably agreeable reply. It is not possible to know precisely what Mrs. Shandy meant. The details of jokes, as I have argued earlier, do not lend themselves to exact interpretation. Our pleasure derives from the incongruity of her remarks and from the fact that Tristram sustains them within a ludicrous context.

The failures of communication are not pleasurable to the characters themselves. But if they don't enjoy them, we do. And Tristram is not above wrenching probability and conventional narrative time to get them in. Consider the scene when Mr. Shandy and Uncle Toby had fallen asleep in the parlor waiting for Tristram to be born. Trim, who had cut down a pair of Mr. Shandy's boots to make mortars for the war games, enters the room to show his creation to Toby. Mr. Shandy is startled awake, and the misunderstandings begin. "Who is there?" cries Mr. Shandy. "'Tis nothing, an' please your honour, said *Trim*, but two mortars I am bringing in,—They shan't make a clatter with them here, cried my father hastily.—If Dr. *Slop* has any drugs to pound, let him do it in the kitchen" (III.xxii.241). When Mr. Shandy learns that Dr. Slop is in fact in the kitchen, he is further puzzled: "Why, I thought Dr. *Slop* had been above stairs with my wife . . . What can the fellow be puzzling about in the kitchen?—He is busy, an' please your honour, replied *Trim*, in making a bridge.—'Tis very obliging in him, quoth my uncle *Toby*;—pray give my humble service to Dr. *Slop, Trim*, and tell him I thank him heartily" (III.xxiii.243). Toby has made the same kind of mistake as his brother. Mr. Shandy had thought the mortars were medical when they were military; Toby thought the bridge was military when, alas! it was medical.

Four chapters later Mr. Shandy and Toby learn that Tristram has been born and that the bridge is for his nose which Slop's forceps have crushed flat to his face (III.xxvii.253). But in order for the reader "to understand how my uncle *Toby* could mistake the bridge" (III.xxiii.244), Tristram must intrude a digression back in time when Trim and the widow Wadman's maid Bridget—are there no end to these bridges?—in their courtship among Toby's fortifications "some how or other crush'd all to pieces" (III.xxiv.247) the model drawbridge. Mr. Shandy loved to tease Toby and Trim about the accident, pretending not quite to understand what had happend but insinuating more than had perhaps actually occurred:

Prithee, how was it then, corporal? my father would cry, turning to *Trim*.—It was a mere misfortune, an' please your honour,—I was showing Mrs. *Bridget* our fortifications, and in going too near the edge of the fossè, I unfortunately slip'd [sic] in.—Very well *Trim*! my father would cry,—(smiling mysteriously, and giving a nod,—but without interrupting him)—and being link'd fast, an' please your honour, arm in arm with Mrs. *Bridget*, I dragg'd her after me, by means of which she fell backwards soss against the bridge,—and *Trim*'s foot, (my uncle *Toby* would cry, taking the story out of his mouth) getting into the cuvette, he tumbled full against the bridge too.—It was a thousand to one, my uncle *Toby* would add, that the poor fellow did not break his leg.—Ay truly! my father would say,—a limb is soon broke, brother *Toby*, in such encounters. (III.xxiv.248)

The associations that attach to each word in this situation are, because of the complex way in which Tristram tells his story, extremely rich to begin with, and because the incongruities of meaning and action are apprehended by the reader in his own ludicrous state of mind, the associations may be infinitely numerous and privately complex.

Mr. Shandy may well joke about amorous disasters. His son, who was just then aborning, was the result of one. All of his own efforts are bent towards regularizing and rationalizing the chaos of passion, the chaos of existence. But in this, as in everything else, he is foiled. The complexity of the physical world, of the action of his own mind and of the minds with which he must deal, forms a set of variables that, while they may not be beyond his ingenious ability to rationalize into abstract theories, certainly are beyond his ability to control in any practical and effective way. *"Pray, my dear . . . have you not forgot to wind up the clock?"* (I.i.2). Mr. Shandy's attempt to defend himself against the passion of his own sexual instinct, "lust" or the "unruly appetite" as he called it (IX.xxxii.805), by regularizing and thus taming it in order, as he would say, "to get them all out of the way at one time, and be no more plagued and pester'd with them the rest of the month" (I.iv.6), this attempt at order is doomed because he must deal not only with his own mind and sciatic body, but also with the body and mind of his mate. His plan of ordering and mechanizing sex by connecting it to the clock merely wound tighter the spring of disorder by creating an unnatural association in the mind of Mrs. Shandy. What feature of his performance, or more likely lack of performance that fateful Sunday night had caused Mrs. Shandy to blurt out her untimely non sequitur about the unwound clock?

What virgin can hear that word, "clock," without blushing? Words may be "ruined" by double entendres: "whiskers . . . in course became indecent, and . . . absolutely unfit for use." "Noses" suffered a similar fate by sexual association. "Are not trouse, and placket-holes, and pump-handles—and spigots and faucets, in danger still, from the same association?" (V.i.414). The fact that words have more than one meaning and that entirely extraneous meanings can be imposed upon words against their strictly denotative meanings is the source of much of the confusion and humor in this novel. Part of Mr. Shandy's pleasure in teasing Trim about his amatory accident coincides with his also teasing Uncle Toby by imposing sexual connotations upon Toby's own passion, military terms. So at this point in the narration of the events of his life, that is, the moment when his nose was crushed, Tristram consolidates around that wound layers of other events, other times, other opinions, layers that act like scar tissue, at once closing and marking the wound.

Perhaps these verbal confusions would be avoided if each word had a single denotative meaning and no other meaning, if, as Tristram ironically declared, "where the word *Nose* occurs,—I declare, by the word I mean a Nose, and nothing more, or less" (III.xxxi.258). The idea that great benefits would accrue to science and to society through the employment of a purified, scientific system of language had been argued in the previous century by, among others, Thomas Sprat, one of the founders of the Royal Society, and, of course, by Locke. But while Tristram was obviously and admittedly greatly influenced by Locke, he does divide with him over the value of wit, which Locke deplored as a form of insanity. What Tristram admired Locke for was the explanation of association, the way ideas are generated in the mind and grow complex by mental association. He praised the *Essay concerning Human Understanding* as "a history-book . . . of what passes in a man's own mind" (II.ii.98), but he disagreed specifically and by his own general practice in writing with the conclusions and recommendations that Locke drew from his explanation of mental process. While Tristram falls victim to the imprecision of language—if only a clock meant only a clock and nothing more, or less—this very imprecision, the very incongruity of the several meanings of a single word, and of the even more idiosyncratic personal associations, this very imprecision forms the gap over which Tristram's humor sparks.

Ignoring Locke's polemic for an ideal and an impossible simplicity and order, Tristram fastens on and embraces the very thing that Locke deplored but described so well, the process of idiosyncratic association that gives words, ideas, and even things an imprecise and utterly personal signification. The weakness, as it may be called, in the word, to accrete idiosyncratic, personal meaning, may in some lights disqualify language from achieving a scientifically reliable description of reality. But this weakness is also the word's power—to charge ideas with personal and complex energy. If words may be fractured into various meanings, if a word's various meanings can be viewed as incongruities, if this incongruousness can be even further enlarged by private allusiveness, then Tristram has here, if and as he wills it, the perfect materials if not for scientific discourse, then for incorporation into the ludicrous context. If words, like bodies, may be wounded and encrusted with layers of scar tissue, if everything may be fractured by accident, if time itself may be cut and hemmed and stitched up at will, Tristram transforms these accidents into pleasure, by wilfully laughing, indeed by revelling in that characteristically, definitively, and totally human state of mind which celebrates pleasure out of pain.

The comic idea comes trailing its painful and often ghastly and bloody associations. But it is the will of the narrator that conspicuously forces and keeps this material within a comic context. The most notable feature of this willfulness is Tristram's manipulation of the temporal surface as he rearranges the patchwork puzzle of historical and autobiographical materials into the seamless tapestry of the idealized presentness of fantasy time. Sterne has given us the details of the life of a dying man as they flash through his consciousness—but it is a consciousness ever attuned to the comic context in which these details are collated for the sake only of the pleasure of laughter. Within this privileged and healing context, incongruities, disastrous "cross-accidents," and even cosmic contradictions are juxtaposed for the pleasure of a powerful and sympathetic laughter that frees the spirit from the narrow grip of words and even of time itself.

CHAPTER SIX

As You Like It:
The Context of Dramatic Comedy

THE GREAT THEMES of comedy—pleasure transmuted out of pain, order out of chaos, harmony out of conflict—are imaged in Shakespeare's *As You Like It*. Orlando's opening speech contains parallel structures that set up incongruities, the ultimate resolution of which alludes to these great comic themes.

Thomas Lodge, author of Shakespeare's source, *Rosalynde or Euphues' Golden Legacy* (1590), uses parallelism seemingly as a habit. Saladyne, envious, plans to keep his younger brother, Rosader, ignorant and helpless, "and though hee be a Gentleman by nature yet forme him anew, and make him a peasant by nourture." Here is Rosader's lament:

> why should I that am a Gentleman borne, passe my time in such unnaturall drudgerie? . . . nature hath lent me wit to conceive, but my brother denied me arte to contemplate: I have strength to perform any honorable exployte, but no libertie to accomplish my vertuous indevours: those good partes that God hath bestowed upon me, the envie of my brother doth smother in obscuritie: the harder is my fortune, and the more his frowardnesse.[1]

Lodge's parallels are simple and generalized, almost mechanical, a word on one side virtually demanding a similar word on the other: "wit to conceive" . . . "art to contemplate"; "strength to performe" . . . "libertie to accomplish."

Shakespeare's parallel structures are more obviously well wrought. But why? Because Shakespeare is the better artist? Because the poetry of drama gives a larger license to linguistic structures, even to passages like Orlando's opening speech? There are satisfactory answers to these large questions. But I will begin small and notice at first only the remarkable fact that Shakespeare has Orlando begin the comedy in this highly wrought parallel style which Orlando never displays again throughout the entire play. It may be that Orlando here is shown driven to a higher state of poetic and emotional passion than he achieves at any other time in his life. But biographically that cannot be true. More likely, and coincident to my contextual view of comedy, Orlando here speaks not only to express his deep feelings about the injustice of his personal situation, but also to help Shakespeare solve his own, more compelling artistic problem about how to begin this comedy on the right note.

All comedy, even the meanest joke, must establish a context of ludicrousness in which the incongruities may yield laughter, or the pleasure which is associated with laughter. The actor need not elicit actual laughter from Orlando's opening speech. Perhaps no actor, unless he dressed like a clown, could extract laughs from the incongruities presented there. But this is not to go to the other extreme and say that he should read them straight, solely for the pathos of brotherly injustice which is there. The comic actor has a doubled and conflicting responsibility, for Orlando does not yet know that he is in a comedy, and yet we must know that he is in one. When Orlando searches for parallel images, he is seeking the language to express his pain and anger. And yet the actor who portrays this search and utters this language must somehow reveal to the audience that the metaphors Orlando constructs are not to be taken with absolute seriousness, for Orlando is not a real person, subject to the vagaries and actual cruelties of real life, nor is he a character in a melodrama, subject to the exquisite torture of a tragically fated life. He is a creature of comedy, plotted for happiness, just as we like it. He, of course, does not know this as yet; but the actor does, and so must we, if we are to enjoy the comedy. The actor, therefore, must subtly undercut but not destroy the potential realism of Orlando's speech. He certainly must not read through this speech with a kind of tragic pontification. Rather, he must show Orlando searching for metaphors and enjoying the wit when he finds them.

Consider Orlando's comparison of Oliver's unequal treatment of the two younger brothers: "My brother Jaques he keeps at school"; "for my part, he keeps me rustically at home."[2] There is here a very slender pun on the double—positive and negative—meanings of "keep": to nurture and to restrain. The actor must show Orlando noticing the pun and then reaching out for new language that amplifies, punches up, this slight incongruity: "or, to speak more properly, stays me here at home unkept" (7–8). So a person may be kept from being nurtured. This pun must be seen by the audience to entertain Orlando and to rush him into an example, and an even further leap of wit: "for call you that keeping for a gentleman of my birth, that differs not from the stalling of an ox?" (9–10). Orlando is, of course, trying to express his own pathetic condition and to satirize his brother at the same time. For these purposes, "stalling" and "ox" are useful negative deflections from the positive associations of "keeping" and "gentleman." They are more concrete and vivid, and the disparity they introduce is certainly larger than that, for example, between "keep" and "stay."

It is not, as I have argued earlier, a question of how wide the incongruity reaches before we call an apt metaphor ludicrously incongruous. The fact of incongruity is not of itself ludicrous or anything else. A single incongruity is subject to any and all kinds of emotional coloration, depending upon its context. The functional element of comedy is the ludicrous context which is characterized by a corresponding willingness in the audience to accept the offered incongruity amorally, irrationally, and without work, specifically for laughter or that pleasure associated with laughter. Once the ludicrous context is established, it does not matter whether the range of disparity within the incongruity is wide or narrow. In such a context, otherwise perfectly apt metaphors would appear funny. It is true that wide disparity, while it is not a necessary cause of laughter, can be a factor in the establishment of the ludicrous context. For wide disparity, that is, wide incongruity, creates interpretational difficulty and calls attention to the fact of context. It raises the question, "what is meant?" or, "in what context am I to begin my search for an answer?"

Viewing the parallel opposites of "keeping for a gentleman" and "stalling of an ox" within the context of satire and complaint immediately yields a satisfactory and conventional interpretation of the metaphor, for in satire and complaint, inversions like this are conventional and typical. And certainly, *from Orlando's point of view,* that is the context in which he speaks. But the actor who expresses only this one point of view, as I said, completes only half of his job, for he must also convey the comic context which is *the author's point of view* and, one hopes, the audience's. For that purpose, the actor must, on his own, slightly undercut the obvious context of satire and complaint. In effect, the actor must deliver a kind of comic wink at the audience while Orlando talks on in all seriousness—so as to indicate that while the troubles may appear devastating, all will end well. Thus, while "stalling of an ox" serves Orlando's purpose by attacking Oliver's conscious neglect, it may also be used to undercut the seriousness of the satiric context. As a broad hint, for example, the burdened beast itself may be heard to grunt offstage. The scene, after all, does take place in the orchard of a country estate. Or, the sound may precede Orlando's analogy, may be observed, as it were, to thrust the metaphor into his searching mind, in effect mechanizing or automatizing his poetic search.

Even if no sounds were made, the incongruity of this complaint from the stable may be played for a wild comic effect, as this "gentlemen of . . . birth" can find no more apt metaphors for his existence than derive from the stable and dunghill. For while he can imitate the superficial structure of poetry, and while he has a knack for structural parallelism and the technique for metaphor, he does not have (and why should he, "rustically" kept and uneducated as he is), the matter of poetry and the essential experience of "a gentleman of . . . birth." The best images he can find for his conscientiously poetic structure are barnyard images. So the actor might well suggest by stress, at Orlando's expense, the pretension of the phrase, "gentleman *of my birth*" (my italics), against which the stalled ox would stand out all the more vivid and accusing. For even though the syntax literally divides the well-born Orlando and his imaged ox, the parallel structure nevertheless leaves the subtle impression of similarity. And, of course, that is what Shakespeare means, for while Orlando is pathetic and satiric about his bestial condition, full of outrage against his brother, it is because he is much like an ox, worse off even than Oliver's "animals on his dunghills" (I.i.14–15)—and this is the man who is to be educated to the ways of love, refined and transformed by them, so that he will come to place emphasis more upon being a true gentleman than upon mere status, the "gentleman of my birth."

We come to the essential theme of the play both ways, from the point of view of satire and injustice, and from the point of view of the ludicrous context, but it is a more stimulating way, and a way necessary for comedy, to appreciate the potential for immediately establishing a ludicrous context in even this, the apparently straightforward opening speech. This speech must, as it does, develop a straightforward exposition of Orlando's dramatic situation, but it also can, and does, support the ludicrous context by employing an incongruity between syntax and sense. Thus, the syntactic parallels, which are nowhere characteristic of Orlando's normal expression, and the barnyard diction create a break in decorum between style and content, an incongruity that serves purposes other than simple exposition and character development.

Words in a ludicrous context are not restricted to exposition, to only those meanings that promote rational discursive understanding of prose. And even more than the wider breadth of meanings allowed in poetry, the ludicrous context permits *any* meanings that evoke laughter or the pleasure associated with laughter. For example, when Orlando quite seriously compares himself with rude peasants, beasts of the field, oxen, horses, animals on the dunghill, he is sincere in his polemic, though the actor may wish to bring out the verbal irony in these metaphors, the unconscious self-mockery. The actor may wish to give these images comic emphasis by calling them out from the mere discursive logic of contrast. He may choose, for example, to portray Orlando as unconsciously burping, fist to chest, as he develops his complaint against his brother who "lets me feed with his hinds, bars me the place of a brother" (I.i.18–19). Or the director may wish to have animals sound offstage. In sum, Shakespeare has provided in this piece of apparently straightforward exposition the incongruities and the wide range of imagery that might and should be used to establish the tone of the ludicrous context. It is entirely left up to the actor and the reader to elaborate the emotional color, the context, in which the play is to be seen.

Immediately, we observe the villain, Oliver, from whom Orlando expects some new offence, for he tells his servant, Adam, "Go apart Adam, and thou shalt hear how he will shake me up" (I.i.27–28). Oliver, however, merely and simply greets Orlando, "Now sir, what make you here?" (29). This is an idiomatic form which is used at other

times in the play (cf. II.iii.4 and III.ii.218) without provoking undue
attention or playfulness. So it is actually Orlando who starts the
shaking up, wresting the verb out of its sleepy colloquialism and
hurling it back sharp and quick and full of insult and high-pitched
petulance, an extemporaneous and punning retort, at his baffled
brother. What do I make? "Nothing. I am not taught to make anything" (30). Oliver, not slow to anger, takes up this play on words,
and throws the dart back with an even better, because it is a more
inventive, pun: "What mar you then sir?" (31). If the performance
is to succeed, get off on a good footing, this line must achieve a comic
effect, even if it is only the kind of groan which is frequently the
recognition sign for puns.

I have said before that it is not possible completely to understand
the logic of any joke, for the ludicrous context depends upon apprehending the incongruity in a state of mind characterized by irrationality, amorality, and the absence of real work. The ludicrous context
does not reward conscious, decorous, or conscientiously rational solutions to the offered incongruity. So there is no single ludicrous
meaning in this make-you/mar-you punning repartee. We may, for
example, respond to the ease with which one sentence can be completely turned around by an economical sound change. We may enjoy
the economy of this shift, as with the single change that turns a
portrait into a caricature. Or we may respond to the surface cordiality
of Oliver's two questions, how the second, nasty question has the
same syntax (and should be uttered with the same supercilious cordiality) as the first. We may also enjoy the blatant cruelty of Oliver's
second question, ignoring as it does, indeed, glorying in his depriving
his brother of an education. Or we may focus on the consequential
word "then," and enjoy the perverse logic which presumes that Orlando must not just be doing nothing, but must be badly, even de-
structively employed. All of these meanings, and probably many
more, are implicit in this pun, and, as long as we take them in a
ludicrous context, we may enjoy whichever meanings please us.

Shakespeare forced an uncharacteristic verbal humor upon Oliver
and an equally uncharacteristic euphuistic wit upon Orlando within
the first thirty-odd lines of this play in order to establish the context
of comedy. This will be a play in which the victim can cut pain into
the shape of wit, and in which the villain makes puns we might

expect from Touchstone. Indeed, in the next scene, when Touchstone makes his first appearance, he produces an enormous groaner:

> *Touchstone*: Mistress, you must come away to your father.
> *Celia*: Were you made the messenger?
> *Touchstone*: No by mine honour, but I was bid to come for you.
> (I.ii.55–57)

If a pun may be said to ignore the intended meaning of a word and instead call attention to and employ a secondary and unintended meaning of that word, Touchstone's wordplay here denies the word itself and separates it from its discursive definition. It is as if "messenger" has some other, well-known meaning besides a person who is "bid to come for you." The effect of this wordplay, and, indeed, its purpose in helping to establish the context of comedy, is to separate sound from sense, to make the surface of language unpredictable and strange.

The normal, practical context of conversation is here suspended, so instead of a sequence of statement and reply from which the conversants seek to understand each other's meaning, all attention is devoted to playing with the surface sounds rather than to understanding their conventional meanings. This effort to subvert simple communication, this effort to exploit by calling attention to the irrational, irreconcilably incongruous nature of language which normally attempts not to divide but to join spirit to matter, sense to sound, helps to create the context of comedy. Shakespeare calls into doubt the very nature of language. He makes his characters use it at times as if it had no other purpose than to provide a medium for play. The fact that Shakespeare makes hero and villain, gentlewoman and clown conspire to trade sounds rather than sense subverts our normal ideas of dialogue, and imposes a uniform surface of pleasure upon the language of the play—the context of comedy.

The incongruities in the opening scenes of this play do not, like metaphors, have a relatively limited range of rationally deducible meanings. We are satisfied with whatever reason we initially feel to enjoy them, and our laughter or enjoyment is not necessarily increased, in fact, is more likely to be squelched, by increased study or actual mental work. Laughter would also be at an end if we took strong moral objection to any of the materials in the incongruity, for example, if we believed it unconscionable for an elder brother to deflect the just complaints of his younger, persecuted brother with a somewhat sadistic verbal joke. Shakespeare has his characters introduce—and even, in the case of Oliver, forces them uncharacteristically to introduce—these verbally playful jokes at the beginning of the play simply to get us well into the mood for laughter, the context of comedy, and to prepare us for the more subtle, less vocal pleasures associated with dramatic comedy.

This verbal play is purely for the sake of the pleasure of laughter. And to the extent that the words the characters are made to speak serve the unbiographical purpose of causing laughter as opposed to revealing personality, the characters of comedy are lessened by comparison with those of more serious modes of representation. This tendency of comedy towards the fairly obvious manipulation of character, and, as we shall see, of plot also, at the sacrifice of more realistic and more consistent motivation, is not, of course, a fault, unless we mistake these large incongruities of plotting and characterization by reading them in a serious, not a ludicrous, context of mind. When we are cued to move to this latter context of mind, we tend to tolerate such incongruities, large and small; indeed, we value them precisely because when we are in this frame of mind they can allow us the pleasure of laughter. And as long as we receive or are capable of receiving this pleasure, we do not mind, on the contrary, we enjoy all kinds of apparent inconsistencies of characterization and patently artificial manipulations of plot, dialogue, and characterization.

Were this level of tolerance of and pleasure in incongruity not early established, we would never be able later to delight in, rather than quibble over, such larger incongruities as Oliver's reversal of character, the evil Duke Frederick's miraculous religious conversion, Rosalind's mercurial capacity alternately to be deeply moved by Orlando's puerile love poetry and to be vigorously cynical and sadistic in her love debates with him, her incredible capacity to disguise her feelings, and even her appearance, from her lover and her father— in general, the whole, sudden, and miraculous turning of the plot away from despair, rivalry, loneliness, and rejection, immediately into their total opposites, happiness, love, peace, reconciliation.

The comic success of these incongruities may not be attributed solely or even largely to the audience's a priori knowledge of and acceptance of them as being conventional to the genre. The play may not absolutely depend upon such extraneous knowledge. It must be self-sufficient, bearing its own contextual cues, preparing the audience for appropriate responses. So, if the comedy will come later to depart radically from logic and reality, the critic must search early for those cues, even very slight ones, as I have already shown, that immediately establish the context of comedy that determines our later, complete absorption in the enjoyment of the work.

If the mood of punning and banter is not exactly congruent to the more serious dislocations in family and state already described by Orlando and Rosalind, if, indeed, they parody on the linguistic level these more substantial and dangerous incongruities, so much the better. The audience must be reminded that this is not a tragedy or a melodrama. The verbal humor serves to set the matter of the play within the context of comedy. The messenger joke, for example, was introduced by Shakespeare entirely for this contextual cueing. Touchstone should be costumed and played to excite merriment even before he utters a word. At his entrance, Rosalind and Celia are debating the source responsible for the ills of life, whether generic Nature or the later accidents of Fortune. Rosalind is just indicting general Nature with this apothegm, "Fortune reigns in gifts of the world, not in the lineaments of Nature" (I.ii.40–41), when Shakespeare cues Touchstone's entrance. His motley costume and antic appearance must undercut the philosophical pretension of the debate—"the lineaments of Nature," indeed!

While Celia debates the force of Fortune, the player who portrays Touchstone would do well rudely to mimic by exaggerated gestures, making funny the import of Celia's reply, thereby giving motivation for her sharp rebuke at the end, as she argues with Rosalind, "No? When Nature hath made a fair creature, may she not by Fortune fall into the fire? Though Nature hath given us wit to flout at Fortune, hath not Fortune sent in this fool to cut off the argument?" (42–45). Rosalind and Celia push their philosophical discussion, all the while pointing it with unflattering references to Touchstone. Celia ends with a direct question to Touchstone, a conventional salutation similar to Oliver's "What make you?" But Celia's question plays some sport with Touchstone's propensity for wayward wit: "How now Wit, whither wander you?" (I.ii.53–54). Touchstone, however, simply delivers his apparently straightforward message: "Mistress, you must come away to your father" (55). Celia, totally ignoring her father's command, is made to utter a perfect straight man's line in which the only slender motivation may be an emphasis on "you," suggesting doubt that such a one as Touchstone had been charged with the task of delivering the Duke's message: "Were *you* made the messenger?" (56, my italics). But the real purpose of Celia's question lies in the opportunity it provides Shakespeare for displaying Touchstone's perverse humor:

> *Celia*: Were you made the messenger?
> *Touchstone*: No by mine honour, but I was bid to come for you.
>   (56–57)

Once again, Celia ignores her father's summons, and Rosalind this time plays the straightman role by isolating the minor phrase, "by mine honour," thereby providing Touchstone with an opportunity for introducing his witty anecdote on the topic of honor. But even when his foolish story finally ends with an apparently dangerous innuendo against the treachery of Celia's father, and Celia defends her father and threatens the fool with a state whipping for slander, Celia still does not seem to recall—she certainly does not act upon—Touchstone's message, her father's summons.

I do not think that we need waste time probing Celia's lack of compliance with her father's command. This is not *King Lear*. Celia's forgetfulness, like the summons itself, is entirely without motivation or any other practical or developmental use or significance. This matter, like Celia's and Rosalind's equally unmotivated straightman questions, was introduced solely to provide Touchstone with opportunities for his first and second jokes. Indeed, Celia never remembers the summons. Instead, she stays put, this time joining with Rosalind and Touchstone in cracking a series of puns at the expense of the news-mongering courtier, Le Beau—so egregiously, in fact, that the confounded and prevented courtier stammers, "You amaze me ladies. I would have told you of good wrestling, which you have lost the sight of" (I.ii.101–2). They stay so long bantering and bewildering Le Beau that the fact of Celia's forgetting to come away to her father is no longer—indeed, it never was—a real issue, for the Duke himself arrives on the scene to witness the next wrestling match and he never mentions or so much as alludes to his daughter's disobedience.

Clearly, the words and actions that these major characters are here made to speak and perform do not have any purpose that might be explained as even remotely in the service of biographical verisimilitude. Nor do these words and deeds have any extrabiographical function in furthering the exposition of the dramatic situation or the development of the plot. It is evident that these actions and words serve no other purpose (indeed, conspicuously ignore every other possible purpose) than the further development and articulation of the context of ludicrousness necessary for the dramatic comedy. It is most important to recall later when these central characters do speak and act for themselves and for the plot that they were once and may also be again capable of speaking and acting for no other purpose than raising and sustaining the comic context of ludicrousness—that is, for no other purpose than to allow Shakespeare to invoke laughter and the pleasure associated with laughter.

Shakespeare established the freedom of the comic context early in this play largely by means of puns. This kind of verbal wit depends upon the ability to see spoken words as spelled, and to hear printed words as spoken, and to mistake or parody the intended meaning by misinterpreting or changing a word. What the characters pay attention to is the *surface*, the literal or aural surface of what is being said, and they play with this surface, subverting it and the intended meanings. In a sense, then, the actual surface of the play may be seen not so much as colloquy but rather as a seamless texture of verbal give-and-take playfulness. In the instances cited above, it is clear that a line delivered by a straight man—even one who is a principal character of the play—does not share very many attributes that we normally associate with actual dialogue.

We may see this special condition of witty dramatic dialogue more clearly in an example like Abbott and Costello's famous "Who's on first" routine, which depends on the utterly implausible premise that the whole infield of a baseball team has such names as Who, What, and Why. Our pleasure in the quite fictional problems raised by the narration of a simple play in this infield depends upon our acceptance of the premise within a ludicrous as opposed to any other context.

We know that the two speakers, Abbott and Costello, are uttering lines, straight and punch, that have been concocted in advance for the purpose not so much of conveying information, but entirely for the purpose of arousing laughter.

Now while dramatists may call attention to the fact that the dialogue represented on the stage has been previously penned—they can do this by various forms of authorial intrusion, notably dramatic irony— the comic dramatist *always* calls attention to this fact of authorship. It becomes a necessary factor, part of the cueing code, in the audience's acceptance of the ludicrous context. What it also does is call attention to the *author's* sense of humor. For while we may respond to the characters' apparent ability to exchange straight and witty lines, we are aware (especially when, as I have noted above, the content of this banter is conspicuously irrelevant to character portrayal, exposition of the dramatic situation, or plot development) that this witty dialogue has been written by the playwright and not thought up spontaneously by the characters. Moreover, from the author's special point of view, if in serious drama the use of image clusters, dramatic irony, plot manipulation, and other such devices gives the playwright the opportunity in effect to show off, in dramatic comedy the manipulation of the verbal (printed/aural) surface is one such primary means for authorial self-expression. Ultimately, it is not Rosalind or Touchstone or Celia who are funny; it is the play and it is Shakespeare. And this fact is brought imperceptibly, but nevertheless effectively home to us whenever the dialogue becomes comical. It must be one of the salient pleasures of humorous authorship to create such moments, just as it is one of our great pleasures in dramatic comedy to read or witness such moments of verbal playfulness.

What the comic dramatist has to give up by deviating, for example, from strict biographical verisimilitude or from a rigorous representation of reality or from entirely plausible dialogue, he happily gains in the articulation of the context of comedy, which is, after all, the *sine qua non* of his work. For the context determines the crucial emotional coloration he imposes upon the matter of his work. His insistence upon the context is, moreover, that aspect of the work with which he is most personally associated and in which he is most personally revealed. The context is a glistening bubble, fragile and radically temporary, scintillating and prismatic, illuminating the little world within as much as it distorts it. It is a filmy envelope that for a moment embraces a world of incongruity, transforming it for the sake of the pleasure of laughter, and at the same time denying to incongruity the myriad other purposes which it serves at all other times. And it is this delicate surface, sustained and elaborated by the artist, which defines and confirms the very nature of the comic work of art.

It is now time to explore in detail how the comic context, which was necessarily invoked by obvious puns in the first act is, by the second act, firmly enough established to become subject to more subtle articulation. This is a process that increases in sophistication and refinement throughout the play. The particular incongruity I here propose to examine belongs to Touchstone, and is a stroke of wit so remarkable that Jaques, who heard it first, must repeat it to Duke Senior:

A fool, a fool! I met a fool i' th' forest,
A motley fool: a miserable world!
As I do live by food, I met a fool,
Who laid him down and bask'd him in the sun,
And rail'd on Lady Fortune in good terms,
In good set terms, and yet a motley fool.
'Good morrow, fool,' quoth I. 'No, sir,' quoth he,
'Call me not fool, till heaven hath sent me fortune.'
And then he drew a dial from his poke,
And looking on it, with lack-lustre eye,
Says, very wisely, 'It is ten o'clock.
Thus we may see,' quoth he, 'how the world wags:
'Tis but an hour ago since it was nine,
And after one hour more 'twill be eleven;
And so from hour to hour, we ripe, and ripe,
And then from hour to hour, we rot, and rot,
And thereby hangs a tale.' (II.vii.12–28)

Ripeness and rottenness are relative terms, dependent upon taste and personal preference, for there is no precise boundary between them. That a single thing, such as a single moment in time, may be seen as at once both ripe and rotten, is not an unusual idea in this play. Shakespeare has Rosalind play with this same notion two scenes later when she twits Touchstone by comparing him with a "medlar," a "fruit eaten when decayed to a soft pulpy state" (*OED*): "for you'll be rotten ere you be half ripe, and that's the right virtue of the medlar" (III.ii.117–18). Touchstone's stroke of wit on ripe/rotten contains the incongruity that the same moment in time, depending upon how one looks at it, may be compared positively and optimistically to a moment of fruition, or negatively and pessimistically to a decline into corruption. This is an incongruity that appealed especially to the "melancholy Jaques" (II.i.26), who characteristically squints the light out of his eyes to peer into the dark side of everything.

It must, however, also be observed that Touchstone's humor in the ripe/rot incongruity does not lie solely in the fact that a single event may have two entirely opposite interpretations, but more importantly in the verbal playfulness with which Touchstone casts these two opposite ideas into a structure that suggests synonymy—with the added effect that as opposite as they are, they yet sound and look similar. The double incongruity, therefore, depends upon the complex idea that one thing, the passage of time, may mean two opposite things (ripe/rot), which also sound and look like the same thing. The humor lies strongly in the style of expression rather than in the content of what is being expressed. The effect would have been much diminished, if not indeed utterly ruined, had Touchstone changed the lines to read,

And so from hour to hour, we ripe, and ripe,
And then from hour to hour, we grow old and die.

It is, as I have urged earlier, virtually impossible to say what precisely in Touchstone's lines gives us pleasure, but we are told that for Jaques it is not the double twist of one object's yielding two opposites that sound alike; rather his own melancholy seems to identify with only one-half of Touchstone's incongruity, the half-pole pessimism of "we rot, and rot." For Jaques the main incongruity is the disparity between Touchstone's foolish motley and the profundity of his pessimism. Jaques is surprised to find the clown, after his own pattern, a true morbid philosopher. As Jaques reports,

My lungs began to crow like chanticleer,
That fools should be so deep-contemplative. (II.vii.30–31)

The poles of ripe/rot for Jaques are parallel to the way he describes his first meeting with Touchstone: "A motley fool: a miserable world!" (13). For Jaques, the incongruity between *ripe* and *rot* follows the same pessimistic downward deflection as *gay* motley and *miserable* world. Now I am sure that we too are capable of sharing in Jaques' cynical laughter at the clownish Touchstone peering at his sundial (as Orlando observes later, "there's no clock in the forest" [III.ii.295–96]). But Jaques, in focusing on the satire in "rot," has missed half of the potential in Touchstone's witty remark—the double comic twist turning on the fact that ripe/rot incongruously springs from and is equated syntactically with one object, a moment in time. For Touchstone, then, the complete pattern is circular and comical. And while Jaques' pleasure is real, it is only half as extensive as it might be.

I doubt there would be very many readers who would agree with Jaques' biased characterization of Touchstone as "deep-contemplative" (31). Of course, no one would wish to gainsay anyone's innocent pleasure, especially that of Jaques, who has so little of it that after his happy meeting with Touchstone he surprises the Duke by looking, for a change, "merrily" (II.vii.11). But my point remains that Shakespeare goes a bit out of his way to suggest that the reason for Jacques' laughter runs along the melancholic bias of his personality. Thus, Jaques' laughter really echoes against himself and his own gloomy, narrow vision. As Jaques later says of his "melancholy," "I do love it better than laughing" (IV.i.3–4).

Shakespeare's humor is larger than Jaques', and so is Touchstone's. The clown's humor played on many polarities, while Jaques characteristically and pessimistically misinterpreted the comedy as a satiric attack (II.vii.16) containing a "moral" (29) and a "contemplative" (31), or philosophically discursive train of thought. But judging from the excerpts supplied, Touchstone really did not rail at "Lady Fortune" (16), as Jaques said he had. For example, when Jaques reports that Touchstone said, "Call me not fool, till heaven hath sent me fortune" (19), Touchstone is only incidentally observing—and probably not satirizing—that twist in human nature that perverts new wealth into folly. More personally, he is bantering Jaques who had inspired Touchstone's quip with an apparently insulting greeting, "Good morrow, fool" (18). Touchstone denies the title by claiming poverty, for only good fortune makes fools, and he turns the barb against gentleman Jaques, saying in effect, "Don't call me a fool until I'm a gentleman like you." Here again, Jaques has projected his own philosophical bias, imagining that Touchstone is a satirist, when we know that this is Jaques' own ambition, as he indicates when he immediately tells Duke Senior that he "must have liberty" (47) to satirize:

Invest me in my motley. Give me leave
To speak my mind, and I will through and through
Cleanse the foul body of th' infected world. (58–60)

Jaques then launches into a discussion of general and personal satire (70–87). But this is Jaques' interpretation or, to be more precise, his misinterpretation of Touchstone's whimsical humor.

Jaques mistakes the clown's comedy for satire because that is his own nature. He ignores the simple pleasures of life, preferring to satirize the human condition, himself, and all others as victims of an evil fortune. Shakespeare has added an extra dimension in this scene by not showing us the actual first meeting of Touchstone and Jaques, but instead presenting Jaques' biased version of that encounter. Touchstone, from his first entrance, has given the audience the plea-sure of his humor, so the reaction of most of us to Touchstone's wit here in II.vii, would probably stand incongruously against Jaques' satiric interpretation and against his nervously hysterical hour-long outburst of cynical laughter. We are not encouraged to identify with Jaques here or anywhere else in the play. And while Touchstone may not stand at the very center of the comedy, his marriage, no matter how unromantically proposed, does include him at the end in the charmed circle of love, happiness, and social reconciliation. Jaques, still the misfit and loner, exiles himself to the curious company of the miracle-working hermit-analyst and his latest cure, Duke Frederick, a paranoid psychopath, for the time being, at least, in remission. Jaques remains alien to the spirit of comedy; he stands apart as one pole against which that spirit is defined. In the scene I have been analyzing, Shakespeare undercuts Jaques' frenetic laughter by intro-ducing a telling verbal irony in Jaques' words, "And I did laugh, *sans intermission*" (32; my italics), which points towards Jaques' great tour-de-force satire on life and hope beginning a hundred or so lines later

(139 ff.), and ending, "Sans teeth, sans eyes, sans taste, sans everything" (166).

Jacques, quite simply, misunderstands Touchstone's comedy, turning it, as he does everything else, into the univalent voice of the satirist. But comedy, as I have argued earlier in the case of Lenny Bruce, actually embraces the faults that satire condemns. Comedy embraces the insoluble problems, the irreconcilable polarities that satire seeks to resolve into clear moral choices. Jaques' misinterpretation of Touchstone's comedy, therefore, has a special significance in allowing us to observe how Shakespeare has expanded and articulated the context of comedy. Touchstone's ripe/rot dichotomy is, in fact, just one of many such polarities: nature/nurture, feasting/starvation, love/hate, court/country, true identity/disguise, chastity/infidelity, folly/wisdom, etc. Touchstone's stroke of wit is insructive because it demonstrates how Shakespeare has expanded the context of comedy to accept this dualism, even as it rejects Jaques' moralistic and satiric oversimplification of the problem and of the solution.

In comedy, there is no realistic solution to problems, only pleasure in the way these problems are expressed, avoided, or magically concluded. Jaques mistakenly tried to make sense out of the ripe/rot quip, just as he tried to moralize on the slaughter of the deer. He is literally a spoil-sport here and throughout the play, destroying simple pleasures with untimely moral objections (as with deer hunting [II.i.25 ff.]), or attacking pleasant dreams with his bitter skepticism (as in his dialogue on love with Orlando [III.ii.255 ff.]). An embittered lover, he can feel no joy, nor will he share in the joy of others; in the end, he sullenly refuses even Duke Senior's request. So he will not stay to see the others' "pleasures"; he is "for other than for dancing measures" (V.iv.191-92). Instructively, Shakespeare keeps Jaques at odds with the other characters—with Touchstone's ebullience, Duke Senior's fortunate optimism, Orlando's dreamy passion—until finally he expells him from paradise as a source of feeling utterly alien to the comic spirit.

So Jaques is sent on his continuing and, one presumes, fruitless quest for answers to the problem of life: from the hermit and his converts, he expects that "There is much matter to be heard and learn'd" (V.iv.184). But certainly by Jaques' misunderstanding of Touchstone's ripe/rot quip, Shakespeare has shown us that such polarities in a comic context admit of no simple answer or choice, such as that life is simply rotten, or that life is all a ripening. The comic context embraces contradiction, and Shakespeare has expanded and provided some articulation of the comic context to accept this polarity, even as it rejected Jaques' moral, satiric oversimplification of the problem and of the solution.

The comic context does not utterly deny the problems, the polarities, the incongruities of life—it rather turns them towards pleasure. Laughter finds pleasure in the problem of incongruity or of dualism without resolving the dualism itself. Consider the opposition between Duke Senior's practised optimism, which finds sweetness in adversity "and good in everything" (II.i.17), and Jaques' steadfast pessimism. This contrast can provide opportunities for humor, as when Jaques is described as making life worse than it need be, adding new sufferings by grieving over supper, or when he intones his satire on all the stages of life. This is a speech worthy of declamation, so much so that to some readers it may appear uncharacteristically poetic, to such an extent that its presence in the comedy may pose a structural problem as well as a problem of character interpretation. Why is this most quotable and quoted of speeches in this comic play given to Jaques and devoted to cynical pessimism? The elevated style and craftsmanship of this declamation, in my view, are not to be avoided. Indeed, the actor playing Jaques is to be encouraged to give these lines special, even exaggerated emphasis. There ought to be a stunned attentiveness, a kind of tension, both on the stage and in the audience as he reaches his conclusion. But Jaques' oratorical pessimism is already something of a standing joke. For example, when Duke Senior learned that Jaques was reciting "most invectively" (II.i.58) upon life, "weeping and commenting/ Upon the sobbing deer" (II.ii.65–66), the Duke was most eager to view this entertaining spectacle:

    Show me the place:
I love to cope him in these sullen fits,
For then he's full of matter. (II.ii.67–69)

Thus, Jaques' long speech on the ages of man must be viewed in the comic context in which the other characters have already placed his extravagantly morbid philosophizing.

The particular power of Jaques' speech, far from posing problems, is necessary for setting up the explosive visual joke which immediately follows. For even as Jaques is concluding his caricature of life (he just said that he wanted most of all to be a satirist) with his portrait of senility, "mere oblivion,/Sans teeth, sans eyes, sans taste, sans everything" (II.vii.165–66), in staggers Orlando carrying a fainting and starving and speechless Adam, who graphically illustrates Jaques' description. Adam, "almost fourscore" (II.iii.71), looks older than his age ("Though I look old, yet I am strong and lusty" [II.iii.47]), and he is, indeed, sans teeth ("I have lost my teeth" [I.i.82–83]). How is an actor to play and an audience to respond to the correspondences between Adam's appearance and Jaques' satire on senility? And how are we to react to the incongruously opportune juxtaposition of Jaques' riveting conclusion and the entrance, or rather the bearing-in, of Adam?

The actors, of course, have everything to do with how the scene is played—for laughs or for tears, or for both. Shakespeare does not elaborate on his bare stage directions. But we know that he has never allowed Jaques to speak without having his speech undercut by other characters. The occasion for Jaques' outburst this time is Duke Senior's characteristically optimistic comment on Orlando's tale of woe and starvation. The Duke observes to Jaques that suffering is a universal human experience, implying that Jacques is too self-centered and takes suffering too personally: "Thou seest, we are not all alone unhappy" (II.vii.136). The Duke radically and habitually finds another happy use for adversity—this time, someone else's adversity—pointing up the consoling moral that Jaques ought to see in the suffering of Orlando and Adam a solace in that

This wide and universal theatre
Presents more woeful pageants than the scene
Wherein we play in. (II.vii.137–39)

The same dualism that had existed earlier is once again created, consisting of the Duke's looking on the bright side of reality and Jaques' reflexive peering into the dark. The actor who plays Adam may push the conclusion of Jaques' contribution to this debate toward any number of emotional colorations, of which laughter is only one.

But laughter, in my view, is the correct and necessary response, for Jaques' and the Duke's relationship is already seen within a humorous context. Moreover, it is characteristic for comedy to deal with duality by avoiding it and taking pleasure from it.

It would be all too easy for Adam to be played seriously, that is, to wait respectfully, like a messenger in an opera, until the effect of a grand aria has had time to be appreciated, and then to speak when bid. Now while Adam is certainly not disrespectful, there is no reason to assume that Shakespeare intended that this scene should be the single place in the entire comedy where Jaques' obsessively morbid wit should be treated with respect when nowhere else are his words received with anything but contempt or at best the knowing smile bestowed only upon the harmlessly insane. In this case, the incongruity can be established without any grain of abrasive intention on Adam's part, for he is nearly unconscious with fatigue and hunger. So he may, without imputation of evil motive, hang a ludicrously heavy burden upon Orlando, who staggers with exaggerated strategies to preserve his precarious balance. Adam may be seen to gape with an exaggerated slackness of jaw, or to goggle and roll his eyes up, faintingly. These rather grotesque gestures would be all the more effective were they timed to come seriatim, with split-second pauses after the verbal cues in Jaques' last line: "Sans teeth, sans eyes, sans taste, sans everything" (II.vii.166). It may well appear that Adam in his delirium is parodying Jaques' speech in pantomime.

It might also be noted by the audience that while Adam's decrepit appearance would seem to support rather than contradict Jaques' satire, there is something incongruous and suspicious in the utterly perfect and timely fortuitousness with which Jaques' views seem immediately to be confirmed by Adam's entrance. But only an extremely literal-minded and unimaginative actor would utterly misinterpret Shakespeare's comic intentions by playing this scene straightforwardly and for pathos alone. And yet pathos will soon come, when Adam finds his voice and humbly thanks the Duke for his hospitality. So while Adam incongruously seemed at first to confirm Jaques' cynical diagnosis of the last age of man, as soon as he speaks, he recalls us from laughter to our earlier opinion of him. This sudden transition from laughter to sympathy is not a difficult one for an audience to make—after all, the laughter went primarily against Jaques, not Adam.

It may be objected that the broadly comic style of acting that I have suggested for Adam is not authorized by the bare stage directions. But this is always the case. The comic actor, like the tragic actor, necessarily assumes the responsibility, not merely of pronouncing the playwright's words, but of coating them with emotional coloration, in fact, of elaborating the context in which the mere words are to be received and felt. The actor who plays Adam should be prepared to evoke laughter by his entrance at the end of Jaques' speech. He must stand for Shakespeare, who here, as throughout this play, converts insoluble polarities into the generous pleasure of laughter. What is really being debated is the opposite points of view of Jaques and Duke Senior, how one looks on the bright and the other on the dark side of reality. And along with this essential polarity come the related ones of hope/despair, involvement/withdrawal, comedy/satire. Jaques' bitter speech, you will recall, was prompted by the Duke's usual practice of discovering some good in everything. Having heard Orlando's account of exhaustion and desperate hunger, the Duke suggests that the company of exiles, and pointedly Jaques, might count their blessings and be thankful for them:

Thou seest, we are not all alone unhappy:
This wide and universal theatre
Presents more woeful pageants than the scene
Wherein we play in. (II.vii.136–39)

But Jaques will not allow such a happy point of view to stand unchallenged, and thus he retaliates with his satire on mankind. Shakespeare's interest, just as it is the interest of comedy, is not to side with Jaques or the Duke, or even to offer direct mediation of the dispute. The comedian establishes the comic context in which the audience is encouraged to find its own pleasure based largely if not entirely upon unconscious significations linking the offered incongruities.

It would be, as I have argued throughout, intellectually presumptuous to attempt to say with certitude exactly what meaning closes the synaptic connection between the poles of an incongruity received in a ludicrous state of mind. It is the very nature of the ludicrous context to protect the mental operations that go on there—so it is a deliberately guarded and safe room in which polarities are intended to remain open and free of logical and moral resolution. The audience, moreover, themselves participate in and help sustain this conspiracy of secret pleasure. In the example we have been discussing, depending upon how the actors embellish their performance, we may laugh at how Jaques incongruously responds to a mere conversational cue with a declamatory satire that grows into a total rejection of the human condition. So there is incongruity in the disproportion between stimulus and response. The actor may stress this line of humor by exaggerating a progressive enthusiasm in Jaques that grows to the extreme proportions of a vatic fit. So by the end the audience is stunned, and ready to welcome with laughter the appearance of the dishevelled Adam.

Some viewers may enjoy the incredible fortuitousness that supplies Jaques, at the peak of his argument, with a living (or nearly living) proof of his contention. There also may be seen to operate here the curious incongruity of dramatic irony, in that the words a man utters apparently freely and apparently intended to serve only his own interest of personal communication, also coincidentally seem to serve the extraneous and unintended because unforeseen purpose of cueing Adam's entrance. Words which bear less or more meaning than their speaker could have intended can, if placed within a comic context, inspire laughter. Others in the audience may extract pleasure in Adam's gestures, which could appear to parody Jaques' meaning. And certainly there is ample opportunity for sheer physical humor in the mere incongruousness of one man carrying another. Some members in the audience, probably among those in the pit, may also find humor in the incongruity of the role reversal, the servant served.

Now while I am arguing for a humorous interpretation of this scene, and while I am recommending that the actors involved in it should exploit it for the sake of humor, I am not ignoring the important potential here for pathos and sympathy. The turn of mood may very easily be attached to the Duke's suggestion that Orlando set down his "venerable burden" (II.vii.167), with "burden" alluding to the former spirit of physical humor, as Orlando complies with perhaps more than polite eagerness, and "venerable" suggesting a

turn towards sympathy, as seen in Orlando's now obvious solicit-
ousness towards Adam. It is important that this turn of feeling be
made obvious, that one part of the action be clearly in the service of
laughter, and that a turn can be observed towards sympathy, even
pathos. The movement of feeling I have been examining is circular,
beginning with the Duke's sympathy for another's suffering, leading
to Jaques' bitter caricature of the human condition, and appropriately
returning to sympathy again.

The comic spirit, unlike the satiric, welcomes polarity, dualism,
incongruity, in an embrace of pleasure. Nothing more strongly chal-
lenges or supports this point than the problem of the disguises in this
play. Personal identity, for example, may be seen simply as a uni-
lateral fact, or as a complex of incongruous facts, or as a combination
of both. Given the range of potential interpretation, how are the
actors to understand Rosalind and Orlando's treatment of the mul-
tiple disguises which are such a prominent feature of this play? Once
again, the idea of the comic context will provide a useful clue. Within
a comic context, it is easy to imagine Orlando simply accepting Rosalind's antics with her wardrobe, and thinking, "I will woo her in
fun, playfully, by proxy, in surrogate, however she wishes, meanwhile knowing that both of us see through the disguise, yet also
choose, for the delicious pleasure of the playfulness, to sustain the
fiction." This charade frees them to express feelings that might otherwise catch in the throat of self-consciousness.

Orlando was, indeed, troubled by speechlessness at his first encounter with Rosalind at the wrestling match: "I cannot speak to
her," he discovered, "yet she urg'd conference" (I.ii.248). But with
a disguised Rosalind, Orlando is freed to play the lover, to assume
the character and the language of the lover, without having immediately to conquer his tongue-tying shyness in the face of Rosalind.
A similar expedient in Goldsmith's *She Stoops to Conquer* frees Marlow
from his neurotic shyness with respectable women. As he confesses,
"I can't say fine things to them: They freeze, they petrify me."[3]
Orlando had not been a good talker. He was easily overcome and
confused by emotion. His first speech, as I have shown, was a hodge-
podge of angry barnyard metaphors that actually rebound humorously against his justifiable rage. When he cannot trade banter on
this emotional subject with his brother, out of frustration he lunges

for the throat. When he sees and loves Rosalind, his emotions again render him speechless, "a quintain, a mere lifeless block" (I.ii.241). So Rosalind's transparent disguise actually frees him from the self-conscious constraints of reality and allows him to fantasize out loud, to act, to practice, and to become accustomed to these new and troublesome emotions. This is actually a psychical version of the play-within-the-play motif, and it is used here by Rosalind and Orlando for essentially comedic purposes.

Rosalind's see-through disguise allows Orlando to transfer his state of mind from the constrictions, confusions, and self-conscious inhibitions of reality to a liberating, hypothetical, playful context that frees his bound-up emotions on the wings of love. "If"—Touchstone's liberating word—"if" you were Rosalind, then this is what I would say to you. What a delicious secret pleasure it is to know that she is absent (freeing his tongue), and yet present (to hear what words his love might take). Present and not present—happy incongruity! This is the same condition as wit and double entendre—to allude to sex and to pretend ignorance of the bawdy allusion. But, as with verbal wit, so here with the disguise, the ignorance must positively appear as pretence, as a hypothetical condition, for actual ignorance is the context not of the witty lover but of the dunce. So it is essential to the comic context that Orlando and Rosalind show the audience that they both know the secret of their true identities but prefer for the pleasure of the charade to pretend ignorance. For the comic context to be sustained, the duplicity must be seen through not only by the audience but by Orlando and Rosalind as well. Thus, Orlando speaks to Ganymede as if he were speaking to Rosalind, yet showing that he knows it is really Rosalind all the while.

Shakespeare constructs the plot entirely for the purpose of allowing an otherwise tongue-tied Orlando to express his feelings to Rosalind. Orlando's shyness can be accounted for in realistic, biographical terms. He does, after all, have the training and the education of a peasant. So he is naturally puzzled and daunted by his surprising passion for the stately Rosalind, the old Duke's daughter and a favorite of the present court—a person and a female person at that who is hopelessly exalted above Orlando's station and education. Orlando, therefore, who was tongue-tied in Rosalind's presence, must be pleased to be given the opportunity to break silence and to express his constrained passion to the ingratiating Ganymede, who from "the first time that I ever saw him,/Methought he was a brother" to Rosalind (V.iv.28–29). Thus, Orlando's painfully inexpressible love for Rosalind, and Ganymede's unaccountable resemblance to his beloved, seem to provide a line of realistic motivation for Orlando's ready participation in Ganymede's proposal of a love cure by means of a charade.

Similarly, we can, if we wish, also discover a realistic line of motivation in Rosalind's offer of the charade. She is in a man's costume to protect her and Celia from assault. When, in the forest, she unexpectedly comes across the shy young wrestler who had made such an impression upon her at Court, she could have given this fellow exile the wink and found a strong protector (he won the wrestling match), albeit a silent lover (he did not excel in love talk). It is quite possible to view her decision to remain in her manly costume as part of a reasonable strategy, as serving a lover's selfish purpose in bringing out Orlando.

While a kind of possibly reasonable line of motivation may be extracted from the evidence Shakespeare provides, there are still such glaring illogicalities present as to disqualify normal biographical analysis. In order to sustain the biographical interpretation, we must presume Orlando to be a kind of oaf. But we can avoid this conclusion and yield a richer interpretation if we see Orlando as immediately piercing the disguises, yet choosing to participate in them. We experience a more complicated scene, the spectacle of an otherwise shy man accepting the implicit pleasures offered by a situation in which he notes that his beloved, pretending to be a male, offers to become his friend for the purpose of pretending to be his beloved.

Orlando's accession to the double charade is the first sign of his true wit and is more meaningful than any of the apparent tests of his love required by his pretended/real mistress. Rosalind, for example, seems to count punctuality the prime virtue of a true lover (cf. IV.i.36–50, and 180–86)—and yet Orlando is generally late. Such a love test obviously is nothing compared to Orlando's newly demonstrated tolerance and mental flexibility in sharing in and supporting his mistress' fantasy. Moreover, Orlando also shows his own capacity for creating comedy, for establishing the purely hypothetical context in which incongruities may yield pleasure.

But what about Rosalind's motivation for her participation in this charade? It may be a realistic female fantasy, under the safety of a truly effective masculine disguise, to befriend her lover undetected and thereby become privy to the masculine testimony of the locker room. Such first-hand evidence is much more reliable than whatever information might be gleaned second-hand by pumping her beloved's actual best friend. But Rosalind is not continuing her charade just for the purpose of extracting privileged masculine information. This is not merely a fact-finding expedition. Rosalind is not out to discover whether Orlando loves her. She knows from the start that he is obviously smitten by her. Phebe voices the motto that is the pattern for all the lovers in the play—except, perhaps, herself:

Dead shepherd, now I find thy saw of might,
'Who ever lov'd that lov'd not at first sight?' (III.v.81–82)

Given in Orlando the fact of love, or at least the predisposition to love, what Rosalind is really seeking is evidence of his ability as a courtly lover. Is he capable of any feeling more sophisticated than the silent, slack-jawed, boggle-eyed stare that at their first meeting testified to a passion possibly no more articulate than that of the animals among which he was raised?

Her disguise is her way of offering Orlando the opportunity of proving not just whether he loves her but whether he is capable of loving a sophisticated, courtly, intelligent woman like Rosalind. Touchstone loves Audrey. There is passion of sorts in the clown. But were he to love Rosalind no matter how passionately and faithfully, she could not have him. His station, his profession, his manners, his sensibility—all of these are interrelated—would have disqualified him. But what of Orlando? When she first became aware of her own immediate passion for him, she had no certain evidence that Orlando deserved her feelings more than Touchstone. What her several layers of disguise do is to provide Orlando with a deliciously complex opportunity to make love to her in a witty, sophisticated, courtly manner. And for this purpose it is necessary that Orlando pierce these layers of disguise. And it is equally necessary that Rosalind know that he knows. Of what possible use would it be to Rosalind to bestow herself upon a dunce—a man little wiser at the end of the play than he was at the beginning, a younger son, a fool to his elder brother, and a dupe to his mistress' stratagems. No, while it is possible to view Rosalind's disguise as completely opaque and successful in fooling Orlando, this view has no advantages over the one I propose.

Moreover, the witty interpretation of the transparent disguise is capable of enlarging the audience's pleasure and, by no means incidentally, also of supporting and enlarging the context of comedy. For example, the straight interpretation of the disguise opens the possibility of a moral issue that might tend to suppress the comic spirit of the play. That is, if the actors play their roles in such a way that we, the audience, understand that Orlando really does not pierce Rosalind's disguise, then we have a conflict between one of the defining conditions of the comic context (amorality), and the problem of the morality of Rosalind's duping Orlando. The moral question concerns the motivation for Rosalind's fooling Orlando with the double disguise and also for her seemingly relentless and merciless ridicule of his love and of the object of his love. If the action itself is not innocent, won't Rosalind be tainted by her lie? Why did she do it?

We can save Rosalind from moral criticism: it is true she lied, but she did it to know for sure whether Orlando really loves her. The end justifies the means. And the means are so pleasant! It is a delightful fantasy that she acts out—similar to a woman's wishing to be her lover's best buddy so that she may in that guise lead him into a discussion of his beloved and thereby discover his feelings within this new and otherwise privileged masculine context.

Another such fantasy is a staple of television soap opera—that oft-repeated plot line in which a wife by means of any convenient rap upon the head suddenly develops total amnesia. She remembers nothing, recognizes no one—especially her husband who, since he cannot make her remember him or her marriage vows, if he is to have her at all, must therefore woo her and win her anew. So once again it is flowers and concerts and heartpain and poetry and perhaps finally joy. Surely this must appeal to the viewers as a remarkable stratagem for the regeneration of romance. But what if the woman were only faking amnesia? In any case, the suspicion is unavoidable that such happy advantages might be the result of strategy rather than neurological disease. And what if the forgetfulness really were faked? Sooner or later she would have to pay for this secret power. A moral difficulty would have entered to complicate the previously and apparently simple pleasure of the plot. But yet, even given this original deception and its moral implications, it would still be quite easy to preserve all of the potential incongruities within a ludicrous context—the wife playing hard to get, the husband turned wooer, etc. All that is needed is to show that the husband fully knows that his wife is faking and that she knows that he knows, and that both of them nevertheless play out their parts in this happy charade. This is a situation that is potentially highly supportive of the ludicrous context.

In a similar way, while it is possible to view Rosalind by means of her disguises as seriously testing the quality of Orlando's love, this view does turn the hero who will finally marry her rather too much into a fool. It also presumes a possibility of the hero's failing Rosalind's love test—and this is a presumption that really does not or ought not occur in the mind of the viewers of a romantic comedy. So the attempt to force a biographically realistic interpretation upon Rosalind's behavior not only introduces the moral issue noted above and intrudes unnecessarily realistic complications into what ought to be our happy belief in the hero's inevitable success, but also depends upon a false and distorted view of comic plotting, presuming more suspense and uncertainty than ever really exists in romantic comedy. But as in the case of the amnesia plot, the complications occasioned by the fakery and disguise disappear when it is made clear that both parties are aware of the trickery and nevertheless both choose to act out their complex double roles. Viewing Shakespeare's play in this light preserves the inevitability of the comic ending, removes any moral objections to Rosalind's character, and saves Rosalind's worthy future husband from the ranks of folly.

While the idea of a transparent deception removes the above-noted obstacles to a successfully comedic rendition of the play, it also offers positive support towards that goal. Let us examine Act III, scene ii, when Rosalind and Orlando first meet in the Forest of Arden. Rosalind has just learned that the writer of the love verses is, indeed, Orlando. Her immediate and feminine reaction is a natural lover's anxiety about her clothes: "Alas the day, what shall I do with my doublet and hose?" (215–16). While it would have been perfectly reasonable for her, since she is safely within the precincts of the Forest of Arden, having available her own father's protection, now to drop her masculine disguise which was assumed to prevent assault, she still does not reveal her identity. Indeed, when immediately Jaques and her beloved Orlando appear, Rosalind's mind is all for continued secrecy, as she wishes to "slink by" (248) and observe him privately. By means of eavesdropping she is privileged to hear what must have greatly satisfied her curiosity—Orlando actually speaking, and speaking with some degree of wit and self-assurance. What she overhears is Jaques and Orlando trading insults with a kind of bantering "nimble wit" (271). Her pleasure in hearing Orlando speak under the stimulation of ridicule apparently gives her an idea that might serve to provoke him to speech in her presence as well: "I will speak to him like a saucy lackey and under that habit play the knave with him" (290–92). Tongue-tied and apparently witless with her at court, Orlando finds his voice and his wit when lashed by Jaques' sharp tongue. Insult and innuendo are stimulants, arousing anger, or in some cases, more interesting responses. Rosalind seems to have learned something of use to her in observing Orlando's bantering exchange with Jaques.

From her place of hiding, Rosalind calls out to Orlando, "Do you hear, forester?" (292). The distance between them must be great enough to make the question meaningful. The distance is such that Orlando can hear "very well" (293), but perhaps not see so well. He turns to the voice: "What would you?" (293). There is no recognition yet. Rosalind comes forward to say what she wants: "I pray you, what is't o'clock?" (294). Orlando must be made now to take special notice of his questioner because of the incongruity of the question. It is a courtly not a country question, for, as Orlando points out, "there's no clock in the forest" (295–96). There is the further incongruity of a perfectly and inappropriately courtly question asked by a curiously "pretty youth" (328) strangely dressed in country garb. In asking the time, Rosalind has given an extremely obvious come-on line, and one utterly inappropriate to her uncourtly costume and place. Orlando observes the incongruity and shows that he has observed it. What else has he also observed?

This is exactly the moment to let the audience know that Orlando is at least suspicious about his new companion. They are now face to face. Rosalind, having purposely provided verbal clues to her disguise which have been duly noted by Orlando, now close to her lover, replies to his suspicious recognition of her first incongruity by supplying another, more blatant verbal clue. So there's no clock in the forest? "Then there is no true lover in the forest, else sighing every minute and groaning every hour would detect the lazy foot of Time, as well as a clock" (297–99). Rosalind's "no true lover" syntactically parodies Orlando's "no clock." The love duel of wit has begun. The word "lover" must be seen to pierce Orlando. The surface is banter, but the recognition has already occurred. Orlando's "no clock" shows that he is at least suspicious and probably fully and teasingly aware of his companion's true identity. And Rosalind's "no true lover" shows that she has accepted his teasing recognition by replying in kind: If she is no country boy, then he is no true lover, for where are his sighs?

A reader or an actor may prefer to read the above lines without the implicit recognition that I see in them. But that way the wit would have less point, would be devoid of the conscious innuendo and the conscious love teasing that I see. Orlando is not a fool. In recognizing Rosalind and in participating in the playfulness of the disguise, he finds he can make conscious, witty love to her, repairing precisely the deficiency he earlier displayed in Act I. We now see them both in a new light—as comic dramatists in a dramatic comedy of their own, having their own private joke. Characters in a comedy, but also authors of their own private comedy, they conspire between themselves alone to establish their own comic context within the larger comic context of the whole play.

Their conversation, they now understand, may be viewed in several lights. After the recognition, their talk concerns the relativity of time, but as interesting as that topic may be, its real value within the privileged comic context concerns the riddling style rather than the philosophical content. This kind of juvenile wit makes little sense unless it is understood within the limited comic context as playful fun-talk, in which Orlando graciously asks the appropriate straight-man questions, allowing Rosalind to show off her witty answers. The act of riddling itself effects a ludicrous context. The riddling question is not a real question, but one asked for the obvious purpose of arousing laughter. The straight man, Orlando, who helpfully asks the required questions—"Who ambles Time withal?" (312), "who doth he trot withal?" (306), etc.—already demonstrates a tolerance for his mistress' fantasy and whim. The straight man questions are no more real than are Rosalind's riddling answers. They belong not to the context of real conversation, but to the specialized, artful context of comedy. And each participant's willingness in his own way to sustain this context is far more significant than the actual content of what they say.

When Rosalind completes her set piece, Orlando turns the conversation towards Rosalind with his probing questions: "Where dwell you pretty youth?" (328) and "Are you native of this place?" (331). Rosalind had just teased Orlando with her philosophical riddles. Now he suddenly turns: since she's so smart, let's see how *she* answers some questions. Orlando is playing with her, teasing her: "Your accent is something finer than you could purchase in so removed a dwelling" (333–34). Rosalind must immediately concoct an answer that must do two contradictory things. She must invent a lie that will support her disguise and put Orlando off and at the same time lead him on. The lie about having been educated by an antifeminist uncle does just that. So Rosalind teases him for being love-possessed and also for not loving deeply enough, and she offers to cure him if he would only woo her. The arrangement proves agreeable to both. By this unspoken agreement, Orlando, in effect, says to Rosalind, "if you want me to think of you as impersonating a country boy impersonating Rosalind, then not only am I happy to please your whim, but I too will enjoy the wit of the charade. And I will not be offended by your satire upon womankind in general, upon Rosalind in particular, or even upon me. I will instead respond with good humor and, beneath the layers of disguise, I will make love to you in earnest while maintaining the surface pleasantries. And my part in this playful fiction will prove not only my love but a wit deserving of yours."

What is required of Orlando in his participation in this charade is a kind of double or even triple vision. He must keep all of Rosalind's characters in mind, and he must invent replies that respond to all of these characters. Even more importantly, he must demonstrate patience in a trying situation, allowing his beloved Rosalind to play out her potentially infuriating series of disguises. In fact, he becomes her straight man, allowing her to show off her wit, often at his own expense. If he displays wit, it is the wit of the straight man, the sparkle-eyed recognition of being in the presence of wit, supporting it, encouraging it, and allowing it to achieve its effect.

Rosalind's wit is a teasing wit: "There is a man haunts the forest that abuses our young plants with carving 'Rosalind' on their barks; hangs odes upon hawthorns and elegies on brambles" (III.ii.350–53). Orlando confesses what she already knows: "I am he that is so love-shaked. I pray you tell me your remedy" (357–58). Her remedy, however, is not so pleasant. She insults him for looking good, for not possessing the marks of love sickness—"A lean cheek, which you have not; a blue eye and sunken, which you have not; . . . a beard neglected, which you have not—but I pardon you for that, for simply your having in beard is a younger brother's revenue" (363–68). Orlando's lines, brief, sincere, sometimes tinged with pathos, or a faint iridescence of irony, since he speaks to a miraculous three-personed goddess (Rosalind, Ganymede, and the pretended Rosalind)—Orlando's lines serve mainly the straight purpose of stimulating Rosalind's long tirades or her short, witty one-liners.

"Fair youth," Orlando replies to her satire upon his beard and his healthy appearance, "Fair youth, I would I could make thee believe I love" (375–76). Rosalind, pretending incredulity, launches into her satire on love as mere madness, and offers to cure him of it, "to wash your liver as clean as a sound sheep's heart, that there shall not be one spot of love in't" (410–12). Orlando, arriving late at their next meeting, is bantered thus by Rosalind: "Nay, and you be so tardy, come no more in my sight. I had as lief be wooed of a snail" (IV.i.49–50). Orlando supplies the proper straight question: "Of a snail?" (51). "Ay, of a snail," Rosalind replies, "For though he comes slowly, he carries his house on his head; a better jointure I think than you make a woman. Besides, he brings his destiny with him" (52–55). Even though Orlando has just been reminded of his poverty and unfavorably compared with a snail, he again pleasantly and dutifully supplies the straight line that Rosalind requires to pursue her conceit about the destiny of snails. The destiny of snails? "What's that?"—pause—two, three—"Why horns . . ." (56–57).

Rosalind's conversation alternates between satire and seduction:

"Come, woo me, woo me; for now I am in a holiday humour and like enough to consent. What would you say to me now, and I were your very very Rosalind?" (65–68). Orlando sees an opportunity to get a word in edgewise and to tease the teaser, so he replies with his best imitation of an arch and suggestive leer: "I would kiss before I spoke" (69). To no avail. The straight man is not permitted to seize and hold the cutting edge of wit, for Rosalind has her parry and riposte prepared: "Nay, you were better speak first, and when you were gravelled for lack of matter, you might take occasion to kiss" (70–72). Orlando is either extraordinarily stupid or an extraordinary good sport.

Rosalind springs the same trap: "ask me what you will, I will grant it." "Then love me Rosalind." "Yes faith will I,"—pause—three, four,—and then the zinger, "Fridays and Saturdays and all." Orlando, ever hopeful, "And wilt thou have me?" "Ay,"—zing—"and twenty such." "What sayest thou?" One simple question deserves a sophistical one: "Are you not good?" Gamely, Orlando returns the ball for Rosalind's slam: Am I not good?—"I hope so"—then zing— "Why then, can one desire too much of a good thing?" (108–17). Next, Rosalind has Orlando pretend that he is married to her: "Now tell me how long you would have her, after you have possessed her?" "For ever, and a day," boasts Orlando. Wrong again!—"Say a day, without the ever" (135–38), and she launches into a satire on woman's infidelity that prompts Celia to rejoin, after Orlando has gone, "You have simply misused our sex in your love-prate." Celia continues, no doubt reflecting Orlando's wish to get even, to expose his mistress, "We must have your doublet and hose plucked over your head, and show the world what the bird hath done to her own nest" (191–94).

Rosalind's banter or "love prate," as Celia called it, functions as an aphrodisiac, as a kind of playful, aggressive, verbal foreplay designed to stimulate Orlando's imagination. While Rosalind in the guise of Ganymede satirizes women for their ungovernable sexual appetites, the idea, while ungenerous to the sex, is nevertheless arousing. So the first disguise as Ganymede allows Rosalind the masculine privilege of talking bawdy. And this pleasant prurience and the verbal playfulness in general are precisely the seduction techniques employed by the other lovers (except Oliver and Celia, whose love talk, if indeed any was necessary, we are not privileged to overhear). Silvius is moved by Phebe's witty insults to consider her as a goddess; Rosalind, for all of her outrage against Phebe's lack of love and compassion, plays, as we have seen, her own teasing game with Orlando, whose love and patience are as much tried perhaps as Silvius'; and Audrey and Touchstone sing their love duet in coarser tones of country sarcasm, gross puns, and heavy double entendre. What Orlando acquires and demonstrates in allowing Rosalind her little joke is patience, a flexibility of imagination, and a kind of humorous good sportsmanship.

Throughout, the emphasis on verbal wit keeps the matter, the content of what is spoken, well within the boundaries of the context of comedy. The characters do not so much converse with each other as support each other in their attempts at wit. This effort, I have shown, was undertaken with particular conscientiousness by Orlando in his role as straight man to Rosalind's wit. More important than the particular strokes of wit is the mood which sustains the wit. There must be evident a willingness to play with the mere verbal surface, to offer straight lines, to assist the playfulness of others, and to take the leads when they are offered. What is created is a bubble of pleasure, as brilliant as it is ephemeral, as scintillating as illusory. It is a bubble that is sustained by common interest and may be burst by a single doubt, a single outburst of impatience, mistrust, or anger. What sustains it is an hypothesis, just the sort that I have described as joining Orlando and the many-faced Rosalind: "*if* you are Rosalind pretending to be Ganymede pretending to be Rosalind, then I shall play along and be your loving Orlando." As I have suggested, the spirit by which Orlando supports Rosalind's playful disguise is, in its reliance upon patience, tolerance, generosity, trust, and good humor, akin to love.

Touchstone, who sometimes appeared to say more than he knew, offered in one magical word a clue to the function and source of this happy context I have been discussing. It is the magical, fantastical word "if," which has the virtue, if both sides agree, to compose quarrels and to smooth over the inevitable jars and divisions occasioned by interested parties living in reality. "I knew," recalls Touchstone, "when seven justices could not take up a quarrel, but when the parties were met themselves, one of them thought but of an If, as 'If you said so, then I said so.' And they shook hands and swore brothers" (V.iv.97–101). Here is a paradigm for the social and filial theme of the play. The action began with filial and social hatred, with insult and angry words. But before swords drew blood, the characters were translated to the magical Forest of Arden, a fanciful context in which former experience and old quarrels, while still remembered yet bear not their realistic force. As Amiens praises Duke Senior for using adversity and finding good in everything, "Happy is your Grace, /That can translate the stubbornness of fortune/ Into so quiet and so sweet a style" (II.i.18–20), what obtains is a wishful and conscientious denial of the pressures, the divisiveness, and the limitations of reality. It is a hypothetical context—a what-if context. What if we agree to meet in such a place or in such a state of mind that for the sake of peace and love and pleasure we bar reality. For even in Touchstone's example, what the two quarreling courtiers must do is simultaneously to agree to efface what they both know is a disturbing truth for the sake of a hypothesized peace. As Touchstone says, "Your If is the only peacemaker: much virtue in If" (V.iv.102).

"If" is the context of Arden and of comedy. It signifies and signals a transit to a state of mind predominated by wish and pleasure. As is often the case, one's pleasure depends very much upon how one looks on life, upon what is one's point of view. Duke Senior chooses to find pleasure and content in Arden, while Jaques seeks further matter for renewed disappointment. Even in the wintry wind's cold bite, Duke Senior prefers to find pleasure: "I smile, and say /'This is no flattery.' . . ./ Sweet are the uses of adversity" (II.i.9–12). But Jaques, unable to take the good with the bad, actually seeks out sadness, for "'tis good to be sad" (IV.i.8): "I do love it better than laughing" (4). Ultimately, the context of comedy is initiated and sustained by a willed point of view—a viewpoint that for a time and for the advantage of the pleasure of laughter excludes the rationality and morality of the "working-day world" (I.iii.12).

Even Oliver, whose meanness begins the play, finally falls in with the spirit of verbal playfulness. When Rosalind as Ganymede swoons at the sight of Orlando's blood, she concocts a shaky excuse to keep her disguise: "I pray you tell your brother how well I counterfeited [Rosalind]. Heigh-ho!" But Oliver is not fooled: "This was not counterfeit, there is too great testimony in your complexion that it was a passion of earnest." Rosalind, on the defensive, insists, "Counterfeit,

I assure you," for once relinquishing the witty advantage and providing Oliver a chance for a pointed irony: "Well then, take a good
heart, and counterfeit to be a man" (IV.iii.167–74). The comic context
exists as a presumption and a wish shared not only between audience
and actors but also between the characters themselves.

To use Touchstone's magic word, the characters say, in effect, what
if we accept each other's harmless deceptions as long as their purpose
is in the interest of pleasure. In this spirit of tolerance and generosity
they sustain the context of comedy against their rational understanding of reality. So the characters continue this context until these artful
pleasures of wit and love talk, these pleasures of fancy and imagination have served their purpose as the fore-pleasures that excite a
wish to translate the contextually privileged emotions and objects of
desire into reality. In this way the verbal wit and the doubled state
of mind which knows reality and bars it for the sake of mutual tolerance and pleasure prepare the way for the comic ending, for the
characters' return to truth and reality.

These fantasies of the privileged context are a preparation for pleasure, not a substitute. When Orlando plans the real wedding of Celia
and Oliver, dangerous, real emotions enter his heart and interrupt
his capacity to sustain the comic context: "O, how bitter a thing it is
to look into happiness through another man's eyes! By so much the
more shall I tomorrow be at the height of heart-heaviness, by how
much I shall think my brother happy in having what he wishes for"
(V.ii.42–47). As Touchstone says simply, "to have is to have" (V.i.39).
Pretending to have is one kind of pleasure, a fantasy fore-pleasure,
but beyond a certain point, fantasy is not enough. Orlando has
reached that point; he tells Rosalind, "I can live no longer by
thinking" (V.ii.50). This is a cue for a change of context which Rosalind is quick to apprehend: "I will weary you then no longer with
idle talking" (51). So she promises Orlando real happiness, and he
asks, because now he wants to know really, "Speak'st thou in sober
meanings?" (69). Rosalind promises, and signals the end of the privileged context of comedy among the characters upon the stage and
a transit to real pleasures.

Touchstone had called attention to the magical virtue of "if," the
ability of the hypothetical context to establish pleasure and to deny
the painful and divisive truths of reality. The transition to reality is

accomplished by a series of conditional phrases, as the privileged disguises which had served to obtain a measure of happiness are now dropped: "If there be truth in sight, you are my daughter" (V.iv.117) . . . "If there be truth in sight, you are my Rosalind" (118), etc. In this happy recognition scene, the word is repeated six times in seven lines (117–23), bridging the gap from fantasy to reality. Hymen adds a seventh and most clearly transitional "if":

Peace ho! I bar confusion.
'Tis I must make conclusion
    Of these most strange events.
Here's eight that must take hands
To join in Hymen's bands,
    If truth holds true contents. (124–29)

The transition is from the irrationality, the fantasy context of disguise and confusion, from the strange, magical freedoms and pleasures of Arden to the pleasures, the "contents," such as they may be, of reality. Now is the time for "reason," truth, and reality to "diminish" the "wonder" of fantasy (138–39). In the end, a doubt is raised as to whether ("if") there are any "true contents" or real pleasures in "truth" and reality. Although the comedy ends happily, Shakespeare does raise a doubt about what the future will really bring.

It is a measure of Shakespeare's genius and honesty that he shows here and throughout that the comic context of the whole play and the privileged context established by Rosalind and Orlando in Arden are sustained by concerted efforts of the will and the imagination. Shakespeare makes it clear that the context of the play and the specialized context of Arden are forthrightly unrealistic. Art is not the same as reality. Shakespeare indicates that the happiness of his characters is achieved by extraordinary and unrealistic manipulations of the laws of probability. He is honest to show us the force he had to exert on probability to ensure the happy ending. And now in the end, now when happiness is triumphant, he is especially honest to doubt its reliability and longevity. Do love and happiness require the contrivances of dramatic comedy and the unique environment of Arden? Can love and happiness be transplanted to the rigorous climate of truth and reality? How long can the bubble last? It is a measure, as I say, of Shakespeare's honesty and genius as an artist that he raises these disturbing questions and then leaves them unanswered.

The first words of the play began with remembered pain, the last look forward (a trifle uncertainly, as we see) to the "true delights" (197) of marriage. The privileged context of comedy stands between truths, between the truths of history and of futurity, and opens a bright sphere of pleasure, *As You Like It*.

Conclusion

IT MAY BE as presumptuous to conclude as it was to begin a study of such disparate comic events as I have tried to embrace in one theory. But it seems to me that a theory of laughter worth its salt ought to be able to explain a Shakespeare play and an ordinary joke. The theory, moreover, ought to be able not only to cast light upon the extraordinarily broad spectrum of events that cause laughter, but also to show how these events achieve their characteristic effect. Accordingly, I have offered a new definition: laughter or the pleasure associated with laughter is the result of the perception of an incongruity in a ludicrous context, that is, a context based upon the absence of rationality, morality, and work.

My definition permits the critic to understand more clearly the discrete elements of the comic event and to understand also the psychological process by which these elements are appreciated as comical. It is possible now to think of the comic text as minimally requiring a simple incongruity—not an irrational, or a witty, or a ludicrous incongruity—but merely and simply an incongruity. The definition recognizes that there is nothing inherently funny in incongruities and that an incongruity may just as equally be the material for a physics problem, or for a poetic metaphor, or for a sermon, as for a joke. The crucial point of the definition is that in my view laughter springs from what might be regarded as the periphery of the text, its envelope, its context.

The context, however, is not easy to talk about, essential as I say it is to the textual incongruity's fulfillment in causing laughter, and peripheral as it must be in contrast to the larger amount of matter that constitutes the entire text. The context is not something as physically apparent and as reassuring to the critic as the larger elements of the text with which he is more familiar. Still, the context is not beyond analysis. In jokes, the first kind of comedy that I examined, the context was generally established by a plain statement that preceded the text—a pre-text—such as, "Here is a joke." Thus, the context may be established bluntly, as a matter of fact, and the audience is then left to find the ensuing matter laughable in the quickest and most enjoyable way possible. In larger works of comedy, however, the context is more likely to require at least periodic reassertion, and at best a more characterized and individual articulation.

Analysis of the subtle cues which help create the comic context can help the critic probe to the heart of the work of comedy. In the case of Lenny Bruce, examination of contextual cues—notably hyperbole—yields insight not only into Lenny Bruce's extreme form of comedy, but into the nature of comedy and satire in general. While comedy and satire deal with the same subject matter, human failings, the different contexts cue different responses to the content: with satire it is rejection, and with comedy it is acceptance of those same failings, an acceptance that views them as happily characteristic of human nature.

Just as the comic context in Lenny Bruce's work moves potentially satiric material into the area of comedy, so in *Tristram Shandy*, Sterne playfully manipulates the narrative surface to transform potentially tragic matter into comedy. Moreover, our understanding that the context is the definitive element of comedy helps us in *As You Like It* to discover the provocative similarity between the punning and playful verbal surface and Rosalind's equally see-through and playful disguises. It would seem then that each of the major works I have examined emphasizes one of the three definitive features of the ludicrous context—Lenny Bruce emphasizes pleasure through amorality, Sterne pleasure through irrationality, and Shakespeare pleasure through the subversion of reality and the workaday world.

My aim was to develop a clearer vision into a confused realm of related pleasures. As different in quality and complexity as the various works I have studied here are, they still belong to the same broad but distinct field of pleasure, and appeal to the same broad but distinct state of mind. In exploring the relationship between the comic work and the comic state of mind, I have tried to make more accessible to understanding and appreciation the happiest of the arts, the art of laughter.

Notes

1. Matter and Manner: Theories of Laughter

1. The conservative theory originates, perhaps, with Plato: "there is a principle in human nature which is disposed to raise a laugh," but, he insisted, we ought to control it by means of reason (quoted in Lane Cooper, *An Aristotelian Theory of Comedy* [New York: Harcourt, 1922], p. 109). Archbishop Tillotson expressed his suspicions against laughter most economically, "for a Jest," he argued, "may be obtruded upon any thing" (quoted in Sir Richard Blackmore, "An Essay upon Wit," in *Essays on Wit*, ed. Richard C. Boys, Augustan Reprint Society, ser. 1, no. 1 (Los Angeles: Clark Library, 1946), p. 207. Richard Hurd observed that laughter "obscures truth, hardens the heart, and stupifies the understanding," in *The Works of Richard Hurd* (London: T. Cadell and W. Davies, 1811), VI, 362.

2. *On Poetry and Style*, trans. G. M. A. Grube (Indianapolis: Liberal Arts Press, 1958), p. 10.

3. Vicesimus Knox, *Essays Moral and Literary* (London, 1782), I, 194.

4. *The Gulag Archipelago, 1918–1956: An Experiment in Literary Investigation III–IV*, trans. Thomas P. Whitney (New York: Harper & Row, 1975), p. 283.

5. Shaftesbury, in advocating full and open inquiry into all subjects, had noted the efficacy of ridicule in exposing entrenched and false views, and observed that "Truth, 'tis supposed may bear all lights; and one of those principal lights, or natural mediums, by which things are to be viewed, in order to a thorough recognition [sic], is ridicule itself, or that manner of proof by which we discern whatever is liable to just raillery in any subject," in *Characteristics of Men, Manners, Opinions, Times, etc.*, ed. John M. Robertson (London: Grant Richards, 1900), I, 44. His followers went further, as Anthony Collins asserted, "Decency and Propriety will stand the Test of Ridicule," in *A Discourse concerning Ridicule and Irony in Writing*, ed. Edward A. Bloom and Lillian D. Bloom, Augustan Reprint Society, no. 142 (Los Angeles: Clark Library, 1970), p. 21. A writer for *The Craftsman*, no. 580, April 6, 1745, argued that "*Ridicule* will always be a friend to truth" (rpt. in *The Gentleman's Magazine* 15 [April 1745], 204). However, Vicesimus Knox, in *Essays*, I, 189, countered, "for though to reason was difficult, to laugh was easy." For further details of this controversy, see Alfred Owen Aldridge, "Shaftesbury and the Test of Truth," *PMLA* 60 (1945), 129–56.

6. *On Poetry and Style,* p. 10.

7. D. H. Monro, in *Argument of Laughter* (Notre Dame, Ind.: University of Notre Dame Press, 1963), p. 255, noted that "there is an element of appropriateness in the inappropriate, when it is funny."

8. For example, Monro, in *Argument of Laughter,* p. 235, felt that in addition to "inappropriateness," the formula for humor must also include "freshness," i.e., surprise, novelty, or suddenness. Charles Darwin also included "surprise" in his recipe for laughter in his remarkable book, *The Expression of the Emotions in Men and Animals* (New York: Philosophical Library, 1955), p. 199. Sidney Tarachow, elaborating on Freud's theory, observes that while there is an economy of emotional expenditure in our reactions both to beauty and humor, we laugh because with comedy the process is definitively sudden ("Remarks on the Comic Process and Beauty," *Psychoanalytic Quarterly* 18 [1949], 221). And Joseph Addison, in *The Spectator,* ed. George A. Aitken (London: Routledge, n.d.), no. 62, for May 11, 1711, improving upon Locke's incongruity theory of wit, adds the important feature of "Surprize."

9. *A Tale of a Tub,* ed. A. C. Guthkelch and D. Nichol Smith, 2nd ed. (Oxford: Clarendon Press, 1958), p. 173.

10. *Jokes and Their Relation to the Unconscious,* ed. James Strachey (New York: Norton, 1963), pp. 130–34, 148–49.

11. *The English Works of Thomas Hobbes,* ed. Sir William Molesworth (London, 1839; rpt. Aalen: Scientia Verlag, 1966), III, 46; orthography modernized.

12. *Essays,* 3rd ed. (London, 1779), p. 310.

13. *Jokes,* p. 94.

14. *Jokes,* p. 102.

15. *Jokes,* p. 97.

16. *Jokes,* pp. 94–95.

17. *Illustrations of Universal Progress* (New York: Appleton, 1864), p. 206.

2. The Context of Comedy

1. Paul E. McGhee discussed cueing with regard to learning theory in children: "a 5-year old may report having laughed at a joke 'because it's a joke,' and jokes are 'things that are funny.' If these cues were eliminated, by presenting the cartoon material in a photograph or in person, or the joke material as a standard communication, the discrepant stimulus events might arouse curiosity, surprise, anxiety, or simply confusion, but the possibility of a genuine humor reaction would be eliminated since the child would remain in a reality [as opposed to a fantasy] mode of assimilation" ("On the Cognitive Origins of Incongruity Humor: Fantasy Assimilation versus Reality Assimilation," in *The Psychology of Humor,* ed. Jeffrey H. Goldstein and Paul E. McGhee [New York: Academic Press, 1972], p. 74). On cueing see also Daniel E. Berlyne, "Humor and Its Kin," in *Psychology of Humor,* p. 56 f.

2. Orrin E. Klapp, in *Heroes, Villains, and Fools* (Englewood Cliffs, N.J.: Prentice-Hall, 1962), p. 136, argues rather over-forcefully that the "normal comic function" lies in "supporting social structure" and the conventional proprieties.

3. Darwin, for example, in *Expression*, p. 351, while considering "the chief expressive actions" such as weeping and laughing, as "innate or inherited," thought that they also "require practice in the individual before they are performed in a full and perfect manner." He argued that these expressions are "of much importance for our welfare. They serve as the first means of communication between the mother and her infant; she smiles approval, and thus encourages her child on the right path" (p. 364).

4. Ernst Kris, in *Psychoanalytic Explorations in Art* (New York: Schocken, 1964), pp. 210–11, notes that the pleasure in play "has nothing to do with the comic," but relates to "functional pleasure," i.e., the "pleasure arising from a sense of mastery."

5. *The Dictionary of Humorous Quotations*, ed. Evan Esar (Garden City, N.Y.: Doubleday, 1949), s.v. Johnson and Mencken.

6. Martha Wolfenstein, *Children's Humor* (Glencoe, Ill.: Free Press, 1954), p. 95.

7. *Jokes*, pp. 148–49, 152.

8. "A Clinical Contribution to the Psychogenesis of Humor," *Psychoanalytic Review* 24 (1937), 35.

9. "On the Artificial Comedy of the Last Century," *The Complete Works and Letters of Charles Lamb* (New York: Modern Library, 1935), pp. 126–27.

10. "The Defence of Poesie," in *Elizabethan Critical Essays*, ed. G. Gregory Smith (London: Oxford University Press, 1904), I, 185; orthography modernized.

3. Jokes

1. Ed. Robert Hutchinson (New York: Dover, 1963), p. 35; orthography modernized.

2. According to G. Legman, in *Rationale of the Dirty Joke*, First Series (New York: Grove, 1968), p. 139, "the important and universal elements of the joke have all been delivered before the punch-line is reached."

3. Quoted in Louis Untermeyer, *A Treasury of Great Humor* (New York: McGraw-Hill, 1972), p. 665.

4. *The New London Jest Book*, ed. William Carew Hazlitt (London: Reeves and Turner, 1871), p. 331.

5. This is a condensed form of a somewhat more wordy version appearing in Louis Untermeyer's *Play in Poetry* (New York: Harcourt, 1938), p. 332.

6. Quoted in Legman, *Rationale*, First Series, p. 240.

7. Pp. 52–53; orthography modernized.

8. Quoted in Legman, *Rationale*, p. 240.

4. Lenny Bruce and Extreme Comedy

1. For Lenny Bruce's performances, I use the commercial recordings of his work as well as the collection edited by John Cohen, *The Essential Lenny Bruce* (New York: Ballantine, 1967). Also of interest is *Lenny Bruce, An Autobiography—How to Talk Dirty and Influence People* (Chicago: Playboy Press, 1967).

2. *Ladies and Gentlemen—Lenny Bruce!!* (New York: Random House, 1974), pp. 202–3.

5. *Tristram Shandy*: A Comic Novel

1. *The Life and Opinions of Tristram Shandy, Gentleman,* ed. Melvyn New and Joan New, vols. 1 and 2 of *The Works of Laurence Sterne* (n.p.: University Presses of Florida, 1978), I.vi.9—hereafter cited parenthetically in the text: roman numerals refer to Sterne's volume and chapter numbers, and arabic numerals refer to page numbers in the above edition.

2. *The Letters of Laurence Sterne,* ed. Lewis Perry Curtis (Oxford: Clarendon Press, 1935), p. 99.

3. See his seminal essay, "A Parodying Novel: Sterne's *Tristram Shandy*" in *Laurence Sterne: A Collection of Critical Essays,* ed. John Traugott (Englewood Cliffs, N.J.: Prentice-Hall, 1968), p. 69.

4. Daniel Defoe, *Robinson Crusoe,* ed. J. Donald Crowley (London: Oxford University Press, 1972), p. 3.

5. *Horace Walpole's Correspondence with Sir David Dalrymple,* ed. W. S. Lewis, Charles H. Bennett, and Andrew G. Hoover, vol. 15 of *Horace Walpole's Correspondence* (New Haven: Yale University Press, 1951), p. 66.

6. *Characteristics,* I, 122–23.

6. *As You Like It*: The Context of Dramatic Comedy

1. *Narrative and Dramatic Sources of Shakespeare,* ed. Geoffrey Bullough (New York: Columbia University Press, 1958), II, 166.

2. *As You Like It,* ed. Agnes Latham (London: Methuen, 1975), I.i.5–7; hereafter cited parenthetically within the text.

3. Ed. Arthur Friedman (London: Oxford University Press, 1968), p. 30.

Index